# COOKIE
# SECRETS

D1557698

TIME
LIFE
BOOKS

**Alexandria, Virginia**

**Time-Life Books is a division of Time Life Inc.**

**TIME LIFE INC.**
**PRESIDENT AND CEO:** George Artandi

**TIME-LIFE CUSTOM PUBLISHING**
**Vice President and Publisher:** Terry Newell
**Vice President of Sales
and Marketing:** Neil Levin
**Director of Special Sales:** Liz Ziehl
**Editor for Special Markets:** Anna Burgard
**Production Manager:** Carolyn Bounds
**Quality Assurance Manager:** James D. King
**Pre-press Services:** Time-Life Imaging Center

**SPECIAL CONTRIBUTORS**
**Editing:** Betty Bianconi, In Good Taste
**Design:** Anna Burgard
**Design Production:** Ruth Thompson,
Thunder Hill Graphics
**Proofreading:** Celia Beattie
**Index:** Judy Davis

10  9  8  7  6  5  4  3  2
Printed in China

Time-Life is a trademark of Time Warner Inc.,
and affiliated companies.

ISBN: 0-7370-1117-3

CIP data available upon application:
Librarian, Time-Life Books
2000 Duke Street
Alexandria, Virginia 22314

Books produced by Time-Life Custom Publishing are
available at special bulk discount for promotional and
premium use. Custom adaptations can also be creat-
ed to meet your specific marketing goals. Call 1-800-
323-5255

# TABLE OF CONTENTS

# HELPFUL HINTS

## EQUIPMENT

**Measuring Cups:** For flour, sugar, and other dry ingredients, you should have a set of cups that measure ¼, ⅓, ½, and 1 cup. Metal is better than plastic. Measure liquids in a clear glass calibrated cup with a pour spout.

**Mixing Bowls:** It really doesn't matter what type of bowl you use to mix cookies and bars. It DOES matter, however, when it comes to beating egg whites for cakes—spotless stainless steel is best since even a tiny amount of fat on the bowl will prevent the whites from achieving their greatest volume.

**Cookie Sheets:** Good-quality, heavy cookie sheets won't warp and develop hot spots, and they let cookies brown more evenly with less chance of burning. Have at least two cookie sheets on hand. That way, while one is in the oven, you can be getting the next batch of cookies ready.

**Baking Pans:** Cakes and bars bake slightly faster in glass pans. If you don't have the exact pan size or shape called for in a recipe, use a pan whose surface area is close to the one specified. If you opt for a larger pan, shorten the baking time.

## INGREDIENTS

You'll get better, more consistent results if you use the best ingredients you can find.

**Butter:** Only butter will give a true buttery flavor to your baking. Margarine will work, but the desserts just won't taste as good. Do not substitute shortening for butter.

**Eggs:** The recipes have all been tested with large eggs.

**Flour:** Most of the desserts in this book are made with all-purpose white flour. From time to time, you'll find recipes which call for cake flour, which is a finely ground white flour. If you don't have cake flour, replace 2 tablespoons of flour with cornstarch for each cup of all-purpose flour.

**Chocolate:** Quality is crucial when it comes to chocolate. Never use an imitation chocolate, and beware of chocolate chips that are very inexpensive, as low price is a good indicator of poor quality.

## GETTING AHEAD

Here are a few time-saving tips:

• Make batches of cookie dough in advance. Form the cookies on a cookie sheet and freeze until solid. Then remove and pop them into a plastic bag, sealing tightly. Keep frozen until you're ready to bake. You don't need to thaw the dough before baking.

• When you are in a hurry, bar cookies are a good choice—there's no forming, rolling, or cutting, and the dough is baked all at once.

• For warm muffins in the morning, organize everything the night before. Measure and blend dry ingredients and take the butter out to soften. Have all other ingredients ready to go. That way, it takes only 10 minutes to mix everything in the morning.

## STORAGE

Airtight is the key word when it comes to storing cookies. They will stay chewy and won't absorb unwanted aromas or flavors if packed into an airtight plastic container or cookie tin. Cookies, brownies, and bars will keep up to six months in the freezer, as long as they are sealed in plastic bags. Cover pies and cakes with plastic wrap and store them in the refrigerator, using a few strategically placed toothpicks to protect the surface of decorated cakes. For fullest flavor, bring them back to room temperature before serving.

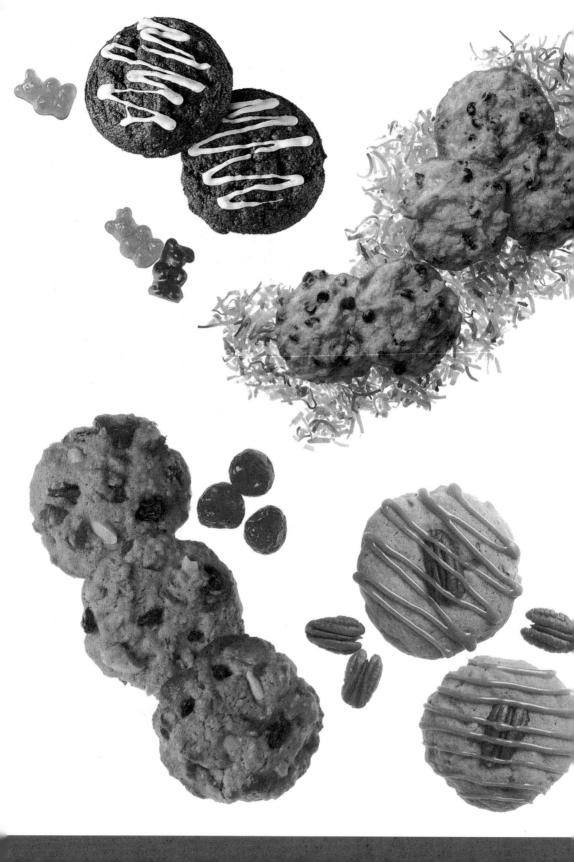

# DROP COOKIES

## Blue-Ribbon Chocolate Chip Cookies

**Yield: About 3½ dozen**

| | |
|---|---|
| **2½** | CUPS ALL-PURPOSE FLOUR |
| ½ | TEASPOON BAKING SODA |
| ¼ | TEASPOON SALT |
| **1** | CUP (PACKED) DARK BROWN SUGAR |
| ½ | CUP GRANULATED SUGAR |
| **2** | STICKS (1 CUP) SALTED BUTTER, SOFTENED |
| **2** | LARGE EGGS |
| **2** | TEASPOONS VANILLA EXTRACT |
| **12** | OUNCES SEMISWEET CHOCOLATE CHIPS (ABOUT 2 CUPS) |

**1** Preheat oven to 300°F.

**2** In medium bowl, combine flour, soda, and salt. Mix well with wire whisk. Set aside.

**3** In a large bowl with an electric mixer, blend sugars at medium speed. Add butter and mix to form a grainy paste, scraping down the sides of the bowl. Add eggs and vanilla extract, and mix at medium speed until just blended. Do not overmix.

**4** Add the flour mixture and chocolate chips, and blend at low speed until just barely mixed. Do not overmix.

**5** Drop the dough by rounded tablespoons onto an ungreased cookie sheet, 2 inches apart. Bake for 18 to 22 minutes or until golden brown. Transfer cookies immediately to a cool surface with a spatula.

### PREPARATION TIP
Drop each heaping tablespoon of dough onto the cookie sheet, taking care to leave about 2 inches between each cookie. As they bake, the cookies will spread.

# Oatmeal Raisin Chews

**Yield: About 2 ½ dozen without walnuts**
**About 3 dozen with walnuts**

| | |
|---|---|
| **2 ¼** | CUPS ALL-PURPOSE FLOUR |
| **½** | TEASPOON BAKING SODA |
| **¼** | TEASPOON SALT |
| **1** | CUP QUICK OATS (NOT INSTANT) |
| **1** | CUP (PACKED) DARK BROWN SUGAR |
| **½** | CUP GRANULATED SUGAR |
| **2** | STICKS (1 CUP) SALTED BUTTER, SOFTENED |
| **2** | TABLESPOONS HONEY |
| **2** | TEASPOONS VANILLA EXTRACT |
| **2** | LARGE EGGS |
| **8** | OUNCES RAISINS (ABOUT 1½ CUPS) |
| **3** | OUNCES WALNUTS, CHOPPED (ABOUT ½ CUP) (OPTIONAL) |

**1** Preheat oven to 300°F.

**2** In a medium bowl, combine flour, soda, salt, and oats. Mix well with wire whisk and set aside.

**3** In a large bowl, blend sugars with an electric mixer set at medium speed. Add butter and mix to form a grainy paste. Scrape down sides of bowl, then add honey, vanilla, and eggs. Mix at medium speed until light and fluffy.

**4** Add the flour mixture, raisins, and walnuts, if desired, and blend at low speed just until combined. Do not overmix.

**5** Drop by rounded tablespoons onto ungreased cookie sheets, 1½ inches apart. Bake for 18 to 22 minutes or until cookies are light golden brown. Immediately transfer cookies with a spatula to a cool, flat surface.

# Eggnog Cookies

**Yield: About 3 dozen**

**2 ¼** CUPS ALL-PURPOSE FLOUR
**1** TEASPOON BAKING POWDER
**½** TEASPOON GROUND CINNAMON
**½** TEASPOON GROUND NUTMEG
**1 ¼** CUPS GRANULATED SUGAR
**1 ½** STICKS (¾ CUP) SALTED BUTTER, SOFTENED
**½** CUP EGGNOG
**1** TEASPOON VANILLA EXTRACT
**2** LARGE EGG YOLKS
**1** TABLESPOON GROUND NUTMEG

**1** Preheat oven to 300°F.

**2** In a medium bowl, combine flour, baking powder, cinnamon, and ½ teaspoon nutmeg. Mix well with a wire whisk and set aside.

**3** In a large bowl, cream sugar and butter with an electric mixer to form a grainy paste. Add eggnog, vanilla, and egg yolks and beat at medium speed until smooth.

**4** Add the flour mixture and beat at low speed just until combined. Do not overmix.

**5** Drop by rounded teaspoons onto ungreased cookie sheets, 1 inch apart. Sprinkle lightly with nutmeg. Bake for 23 to 25 minutes or until bottoms turn light brown. Transfer to cool, flat surface immediately with a spatula.

# Pumpkin Spice Cookies

**Yield: About 3 dozen**

**2 ½** CUPS ALL-PURPOSE FLOUR
**½** TEASPOON BAKING SODA
**¼** TEASPOON SALT
**2** TEASPOONS PUMPKIN PIE SPICE
**1** CUP (PACKED) DARK BROWN SUGAR
**½** CUP GRANULATED SUGAR
**1 ½** STICKS (¾ CUP) SALTED BUTTER, SOFTENED
**1** LARGE EGG
**1** CUP PUMPKIN (CANNED OR FRESHLY COOKED)
**1** TEASPOON VANILLA EXTRACT
**6** OUNCES RAISINS (ABOUT 1 CUP)
**2** OUNCES WALNUTS, CHOPPED (ABOUT ½ CUP)

**1** Preheat oven to 300°F.

**2** In a medium bowl, combine flour, soda, salt, and pumpkin pie spice. Mix well with a wire whisk and set aside.

**3** In a large bowl, blend sugars with an electric mixer set at medium speed. Add the butter and beat to form a grainy paste. Scrape sides of bowl, then add egg, pumpkin, and vanilla. Beat at medium speed until light and fluffy.

**4** Add the flour mixture, raisins, and walnuts. Blend at low speed just until combined. Do not overmix.

**5** Drop by rounded tablespoons onto ungreased cookie sheets, 1½ inches apart. Bake for 22 to 24 minutes until cookies are slightly brown along edges. Immediately transfer cookies with a spatula to a cool, flat surface.

# Soft and Chewy Peanut Butter Cookies

**Yield: About 3 ½ dozen**

| | |
|---|---|
| **2** | CUPS ALL-PURPOSE FLOUR |
| **½** | TEASPOON BAKING SODA |
| **¼** | TEASPOON SALT |
| **1¾** | CUPS (PACKED) DARK BROWN SUGAR |
| **1¾** | CUPS GRANULATED SUGAR |
| **2** | STICKS (1 CUP) SALTED BUTTER, SOFTENED |
| **3** | LARGE EGGS |
| **1** | CUP CREAMY PEANUT BUTTER |
| **2** | TEASPOONS VANILLA EXTRACT |

**PREPARATION TIP**
After the dough is dropped onto the cookie sheet, use a fork to press a crisscross pattern in each cookie. In order to keep dough from sticking to the fork as you proceed, dip the fork in water after each cookie is flattened.

**1** Preheat oven to 300°F.

**2** In a medium bowl, combine flour, soda, and salt. Mix well with a wire whisk. Set aside.

**3** In a large bowl, blend sugars using an electric mixer set at medium speed. Add butter and mix to form a grainy paste, scraping the sides of the bowl. Add eggs, peanut butter, and vanilla, and mix at medium speed until light and fluffy.

**4** Add the flour mixture and mix at low speed until just mixed. Do not overmix.

**5** Drop by rounded tablespoons onto an ungreased cookie sheet, 1½ inches apart. With a wet fork, gently press a crisscross pattern on top of cookies. Bake for 18 to 22 minutes until cookies are slightly brown along edges. Transfer cookies immediately to a cool, flat surface with a spatula.

**6** As a variation, add 2 cups coarsely chopped semisweet chocolate bar or 2 cups semisweet chocolate chips to the flour mixture, then bake as directed.

# Butterscotch Pecan Cookies

**Yield: About 2 ½ dozen**

## Cookies

| | |
|---|---|
| **2 ½** | CUPS ALL-PURPOSE FLOUR |
| **½** | TEASPOON BAKING SODA |
| **¼** | TEASPOON SALT |
| **1 ½** | CUPS (PACKED) DARK BROWN SUGAR |
| **2** | STICKS (1 CUP) SALTED BUTTER, SOFTENED |
| **2** | LARGE EGGS |
| **2** | TEASPOONS VANILLA EXTRACT |
| **4** | OUNCES CHOPPED PECANS (ABOUT 1 CUP) |
| **3** | OUNCES WHOLE PECANS (ABOUT 1 CUP) |

## Caramel Glaze

| | |
|---|---|
| **8** | OUNCES CARAMELS |
| **¼** | CUP HEAVY CREAM |

### PREPARATION TIP

For an authentic butterscotch flavor, an equal quantity of Scotch whisky may be substituted for the vanilla.

**1** Preheat oven to 300°F.

**2** In medium bowl, combine flour, soda, and salt. Mix well with a wire whisk. Set aside.

**3** In large bowl with electric mixer beat sugar and butter. Mix to form a grainy paste, scraping down the sides of the bowl. Add eggs and vanilla, and beat at medium speed until soft and lumpy. Add the flour mixture and chopped pecans, and mix at low speed until just combined. Do not overmix.

**4** Drop dough by rounded tablespoons 2 inches apart onto ungreased cookie sheets. Place one whole pecan in center of each cookie. Bake for 23 to 25 minutes or until cookie edges begin to brown lightly. Transfer immediately to cool, flat surface with a spatula.

**5** Prepare the caramel glaze: Melt the caramels with the cream in a small saucepan over low heat. Stir with a wooden spoon until smooth. Remove from heat.

**6** Drizzle cooled cookies with caramel glaze into desired pattern using a spoon or fork.

# Apricot Nectar Cookies

**Yield: About 2 dozen**

2¾ CUPS ALL-PURPOSE FLOUR
1 TEASPOON BAKING SODA
¾ CUP GRANULATED SUGAR
¼ CUP (PACKED) DARK BROWN SUGAR
2 STICKS (1 CUP) SALTED BUTTER, SOFTENED
1 LARGE EGG
¼ CUP APRICOT NECTAR
½ CUP APRICOT PRESERVES
¾ CUP DRIED APRICOTS, CHOPPED

**1** Preheat oven to 300°F.

**2** In a medium bowl, combine flour and baking soda. Mix well with a wire whisk and set aside.

**3** In a large bowl, blend sugars with an electric mixer at medium speed. Add butter and mix to form a grainy paste. Scrape down sides of bowl. Then add egg, apricot nectar, and apricot preserves; beat at medium speed until smooth.

**4** Add the flour mixture and apricots, and blend on low just until combined. Do not overmix.

**5** Drop by rounded tablespoons onto ungreased cookie sheets, 1½ inches apart. Bake for 19 to 22 minutes or until the cookies just begin to brown at the bottom edges.

**6** Remove from oven and let cookies cool on cookie sheets 5 minutes before transferring to a cool, flat surface with a spatula.

# Chocolate Raisin Cookies

**Yield: About 4 dozen**

2 STICKS (1 CUP) SALTED BUTTER, DIVIDED
2 OUNCES UNSWEETENED BAKING CHOCOLATE
2¼ CUPS ALL-PURPOSE FLOUR
½ TEASPOON BAKING SODA
¼ TEASPOON SALT
1 CUP (PACKED) DARK BROWN SUGAR
½ CUP GRANULATED SUGAR
2 LARGE EGGS
2 TEASPOONS VANILLA EXTRACT
9 OUNCES RAISINS (ABOUT 1½ CUPS)
6 OUNCES SEMISWEET CHOCOLATE CHIPS (ABOUT 1 CUP)

**1** Preheat oven to 300°F.

**2** In a double boiler over hot, not boiling, water, melt ½ cup butter and the unsweetened chocolate. Remove from heat. Set aside.

**3** In a medium bowl, combine flour, soda, and salt. Mix well with a wire whisk. Set aside.

**4** In a large bowl with an electric mixer blend sugars at medium speed until fluffy. Add the remaining ½ cup butter and mix to form a grainy paste, scraping down the sides of the bowl. Add eggs and vanilla, and beat at medium speed until light and fluffy. Add melted chocolate and blend until the mixture is thoroughly combined.

**5** Add the flour mixture, raisins, and chocolate chips. Blend at low speed until just combined. Do not overmix.

**6** Drop by rounded tablespoons onto ungreased cookie sheets, 2 inches apart. Bake for 20 to 22 minutes or until set. Transfer to a cool, flat surface immediately with a spatula.

# Cashew and Coconut Cookies

**Yield: About 2 ½ dozen**

| | |
|---|---|
| **2 ¼** | CUPS ALL-PURPOSE FLOUR |
| **½** | TEASPOON BAKING SODA |
| **¼** | TEASPOON SALT |
| **¾** | CUP (PACKED) LIGHT BROWN SUGAR |
| **½** | CUP GRANULATED SUGAR |
| **1 ½** | STICKS (¾ CUP) SALTED BUTTER, SOFTENED |
| **2** | LARGE EGGS |
| **2** | TEASPOONS VANILLA EXTRACT |
| **½** | CUP SWEETENED SHREDDED COCONUT |
| **4** | OUNCES CHOPPED, UNSALTED RAW CASHEWS (ABOUT 1 CUP) |
| **4** | OUNCES CHOPPED DATES (ABOUT 1 CUP) |
| **2** | OUNCES SWEETENED SHREDDED COCONUT (ABOUT ¼ CUP), RESERVED FOR TOPPING |

**1** Preheat oven to 300°F.

**2** In a medium bowl, combine flour, soda, and salt. Mix well with a wire whisk and set aside.

**3** In a medium bowl, combine sugars with an electric mixer at medium speed. Add butter and mix to form a grainy paste. Add eggs and vanilla, and beat until smooth.

**4** Add flour mixture, coconut, cashews, and dates. Blend at low speed just until combined. Do not overmix.

**5** Drop by rounded tablespoons onto ungreased cookie sheets, 2 inches apart. Sprinkle tops lightly with reserved coconut.

**6** Bake for 18 to 22 minutes or until bottoms turn golden brown. With a spatula, transfer cookies to a cool, flat surface.

# Fudge Cookies with White Chocolate

**Yield: About 3 dozen**

| | |
|---|---|
| **12** | OUNCES SEMISWEET CHOCOLATE, FINELY CHOPPED |
| **2** | CUPS ALL-PURPOSE FLOUR |
| **¾** | CUP UNSWEETENED COCOA POWDER |
| **1** | TEASPOON BAKING SODA |
| **¼** | TEASPOON SALT |
| **2** | STICKS (1 CUP) UNSALTED BUTTER, SOFTENED |
| **1½** | CUPS (PACKED) DARK BROWN SUGAR |
| **3** | LARGE EGGS, AT ROOM TEMPERATURE |
| **2** | TEASPOONS VANILLA EXTRACT |
| **4** | OUNCES WHITE CHOCOLATE, COARSELY CHOPPED |
| **1** | TEASPOON VEGETABLE OIL |

**1** Preheat the oven to 300°F.

**2** In a double boiler, melt the semisweet chocolate over hot, not simmering, water. Set aside to cool slightly.

**3** In a medium bowl, combine the flour, cocoa, baking soda, and salt.

**4** In a large bowl with an electric mixer, cream the butter and sugar. Beat in the eggs and vanilla until just combined. Blend in the cooled semisweet chocolate. Blend in the flour mixture until just combined.

**5** Drop the dough by rounded tablespoons 2 inches apart onto an ungreased cookie sheet. Bake for 18 to 22 minutes, or until set. Cool on the cookie sheet for 1 minute, then transfer to wire racks to cool completely.

**6** In a double boiler, melt the white chocolate with the oil over hot, not simmering, water. Set aside to cool slightly.

**7** Dip a fork into the melted white chocolate and drizzle over the cookies.

# Lemon Poppy Seed Cookies

**Yield: About 2 dozen**

| | |
|---|---|
| **2** | CUPS ALL-PURPOSE FLOUR |
| **½** | TEASPOON BAKING SODA |
| **1½** | TEASPOONS FRESHLY GRATED LEMON ZEST |
| **1** | TEASPOON GROUND CORIANDER |
| **2** | TABLESPOONS POPPY SEEDS |
| **1½** | STICKS (¾ CUP) SALTED BUTTER, SOFTENED |
| **1** | CUP GRANULATED SUGAR |
| **2** | LARGE EGG YOLKS |
| **1** | LARGE WHOLE EGG |
| **1½** | TEASPOONS LEMON EXTRACT |

**1** Preheat oven 300°F.

**2** In a medium bowl, combine flour, baking soda, lemon zest, coriander, and poppy seeds. Mix well with a wire whisk and set aside.

**3** In a large bowl, cream butter and sugar with electric mixer at medium speed until mixture forms a grainy paste. Scrape down sides of bowl, then add yolks, egg, and lemon extract. Beat at medium speed until light and fluffy.

**4** Add the flour mixture and mix at low speed just until combined. Do not overmix.

**5** Drop by rounded tablespoons onto ungreased cookie sheets, 2 inches apart. Bake for 21 to 23 minutes until cookies are slightly brown along edges. Immediately transfer cookies with a spatula to a cool, flat surface.

# Pecan Supremes

**Yield: About 3 dozen**

| | |
|---|---|
| **2** | CUPS ALL-PURPOSE FLOUR |
| **½** | TEASPOON BAKING SODA |
| **¼** | TEASPOON SALT |
| **¾** | CUP QUICK OATS (NOT INSTANT) |
| **¾** | CUP (PACKED) DARK BROWN SUGAR |
| **¾** | CUP GRANULATED SUGAR |
| **2** | STICKS (1 CUP) SALTED BUTTER, SOFTENED |
| **2** | LARGE EGGS |
| **2** | TEASPOONS VANILLA EXTRACT |
| **4** | OUNCES CHOPPED PECANS (ABOUT 1 CUP) |
| **6** | OUNCES SEMISWEET CHOCOLATE CHIPS (ABOUT 1 CUP) |

**1** Preheat oven to 300°F.

**2** In a medium bowl combine flour, soda, salt, and oats. Mix well with wire whisk and set aside.

**3** In a large bowl, blend sugars with an electric mixer at medium speed. Add butter and mix to form a grainy paste. Scrape down sides of bowl, then add eggs and vanilla. Beat at medium speed until light and fluffy.

**4** Add the flour mixture, pecans, and chocolate chips, and blend at low speed just until combined. Do not overmix.

**5** Drop dough by rounded tablespoons onto ungreased cookie sheets, 1½ inches apart. Bake for 18 to 20 minutes. Immediately transfer cookies with a spatula to a cool, flat surface.

# Applesauce Oaties

**Yield: About 4 dozen**

**1¾** CUPS QUICK OATS (NOT INSTANT)
**1½** CUPS ALL-PURPOSE FLOUR
**1** TEASPOON BAKING POWDER
**½** TEASPOON BAKING SODA
**½** TEASPOON SALT
**1** TEASPOON GROUND CINNAMON
**½** TEASPOON GROUND NUTMEG
**1** CUP (PACKED) LIGHT BROWN SUGAR
**½** CUP GRANULATED SUGAR
**1** STICK (½ CUP) SALTED BUTTER, SOFTENED
**1** LARGE EGG
**¾** CUP APPLESAUCE
**6** OUNCES SEMISWEET CHOCOLATE CHIPS (ABOUT 1 CUP)
**6** OUNCES RAISINS (ABOUT 1 CUP)
**4** OUNCES CHOPPED WALNUTS (ABOUT 1 CUP)

**1** Preheat oven to 375°F.

**2** In a medium bowl, combine oats, flour, baking powder, soda, salt, cinnamon, and nutmeg. Mix well with a wire whisk and set aside.

**3** In a large bowl, combine sugars with an electric mixer at medium speed. Add butter and beat to form a grainy paste. Add egg and applesauce, and blend until smooth.

**4** Add the flour mixture, chocolate chips, raisins, and walnuts. Blend at low speed just until combined. Do not overmix.

**5** Drop dough by tablespoons onto lightly greased cookie sheets, 2 inches apart. Bake for 12 to 14 minutes or until cookies are light brown. Immediately transfer them with a spatula to a cool, flat surface.

# Low-Fat Chocolate Cookies

**Yield: About 5½ dozen**

**2⅔** CUPS ALL-PURPOSE FLOUR
**½** CUP UNSWEETENED COCOA POWDER
**1** TEASPOON BAKING SODA
**½** TEASPOON SALT
**¾** CUP (PACKED) DARK BROWN SUGAR
**¾** CUP GRANULATED SUGAR
**⅓** CUP CANOLA OIL
**½** CUP UNSWEETENED APPLESAUCE
**3** EGG WHITES
**2** TEASPOONS VANILLA EXTRACT
**½** CUP MINI SEMISWEET CHOCOLATE CHIPS

**1** In a medium bowl, combine the flour, cocoa, baking soda, and salt.

**2** In another medium bowl with an electric mixer, blend the brown and granulated sugars. Slowly beat in the oil. Beat in the applesauce, egg whites, and vanilla, and blend on low speed until smooth.

**3** Add the flour mixture and blend on low speed until the dough is just combined. Refrigerate the dough until firm, about 1 hour.

**4** Preheat the oven to 300°F.

**5** Roll the dough into small 1-inch balls, place on a cookie sheet and flatten slightly. Sprinkle with the mini chocolate chips, then bake for 17 to 19 minutes (do not overbake; when the cookies cool they will get hard). Transfer the cookies to wire racks to cool.

# Mocha Chunk Cookies

**Yield: About 4 dozen**

**2 ½** CUPS ALL-PURPOSE FLOUR
**⅓** CUP UNSWEETENED COCOA POWDER
**½** TEASPOON BAKING SODA
**¼** TEASPOON SALT
**2** TEASPOONS INSTANT COFFEE CRYSTALS
(FRENCH ROAST OR OTHER DARK COFFEE)
**2** TEASPOONS COFFEE LIQUEUR
**1** CUP GRANULATED SUGAR
**¾** CUP (PACKED) DARK BROWN SUGAR
**2** STICKS (1 CUP) SALTED BUTTER, SOFTENED
**2** LARGE EGGS
**10** OUNCES SEMISWEET CHOCOLATE BAR,
COARSELY CHOPPED (ABOUT 2 CUPS)

**1** Preheat oven to 300°F.

**2** In a medium bowl, combine flour, cocoa, soda, and salt. Mix well with a wire whisk and set aside.

**3** In a small bowl, dissolve coffee crystals in coffee liqueur and set aside.

**4** In a large bowl, blend sugars with an electric mixer at medium speed. Add butter and mix to form a grainy paste. Scrape down sides of bowl. Then add eggs and dissolved coffee crystals, and beat at medium speed until smooth.

**5** Add the flour mixture and chocolate chunks, and blend at low speed just until combined. Do not overmix.

**6** Drop by rounded tablespoons onto ungreased cookie sheet, 2 inches apart. Bake for 20 to 22 minutes. Immediately transfer cookies with a spatula to a cool, flat surface.

# Black-and-Whites

**Yield: About 3 dozen**

**2 ¼** CUPS ALL-PURPOSE FLOUR
**½** CUP UNSWEETENED COCOA POWDER
**½** TEASPOON BAKING SODA
**¼** TEASPOON SALT
**1** CUP (PACKED) DARK BROWN SUGAR
**¾** CUP GRANULATED SUGAR
**2** STICKS (1 CUP) SALTED BUTTER, SOFTENED
**3** LARGE EGGS
**2** TEASPOONS VANILLA EXTRACT
**5 ¼** OUNCES SEMISWEET CHOCOLATE BAR,
COARSELY CHOPPED (ABOUT 1 CUP)
**5 ¼** OUNCES WHITE CHOCOLATE BAR, COARSELY
CHOPPED (ABOUT 1 CUP)

**1** Preheat oven to 300°F.

**2** In medium bowl, combine flour, cocoa, soda, and salt. Mix well with a wire whisk. Set aside.

**3** Blend sugars in a large bowl using an electric mixer set at medium speed. Add butter and mix to form a grainy paste, scraping down the sides of the bowl. Add eggs and vanilla, and beat at medium speed until smooth.

**4** Add the flour mixture and chocolates, and blend at low speed until just combined. Do not overmix.

**5** Drop by rounded tablespoons onto ungreased cookie sheets, 2 inches apart. Bake for 18 to 22 minutes. Transfer cookies immediately to a cool, flat surface.

# Marbles

**Yield: About 2 ½ dozen**

**2** CUPS ALL-PURPOSE FLOUR
**½** TEASPOON BAKING POWDER
**¼** TEASPOON SALT
**½** CUP (PACKED) LIGHT BROWN SUGAR
**½** CUP GRANULATED SUGAR
**1** STICK (½ CUP) SALTED BUTTER, SOFTENED
**1** LARGE EGG
**4** OUNCES SOUR CREAM (½ CUP)
**1** TEASPOON VANILLA EXTRACT
**6** OUNCES SEMISWEET CHOCOLATE CHIPS (ABOUT 1 CUP)

**PREPARATION TIP**
Fold the cool melted chocolate into the cookie batter, stirring lightly with a wooden spoon. Continue stirring only until the chocolate is well distributed and creates a swirled, marbleized pattern.

**1** Preheat oven to 300°F.

**2** In medium bowl, combine flour, baking powder, and salt with wire whisk. Set aside.

**3** Combine sugars in a large bowl using an electric mixer set at medium speed. Add butter and beat until batter is grainy. Add egg, sour cream, and vanilla, and beat at medium speed until light and fluffy. Scrape bowl. Add the flour mixture and blend at low speed until just combined. Do not overmix.

**4** Place chocolate chips in double boiler over hot, but not boiling, water. Stir constantly until melted. Or, place chips in a microwave-proof bowl and microwave on high, stirring every 20 seconds until melted.

**5** Cool chocolate for a few minutes and pour over cookie batter. Using a wooden spoon or rubber spatula, lightly fold melted chocolate into the dough. Do not mix chocolate completely into cookie dough.

**6** Drop by rounded tablespoons, 2 inches apart, onto ungreased cookie sheets. Bake for 20 to 22 minutes. Do not brown. Quickly transfer cookies to a cool surface.

# Carrot Fruit Jumbles

**Yield: About 4 dozen**

2½ CUPS ALL-PURPOSE FLOUR
1   TEASPOON BAKING SODA
½   TEASPOON BAKING POWDER
½   TEASPOON GROUND CLOVES
2   TEASPOONS GROUND CINNAMON
¼   TEASPOON SALT
1   CUP QUICK OATS (NOT INSTANT)
¾   CUP (PACKED) DARK BROWN SUGAR
¾   CUP GRANULATED SUGAR
2   STICKS (1 CUP) SALTED BUTTER, SOFTENED
2   LARGE EGGS
2   TEASPOONS VANILLA EXTRACT
2   CUPS GRATED CARROT
    (2 OR 3 MEDIUM CARROTS)
½   CUP CRUSHED PINEAPPLE, DRAINED
4   OUNCES CHOPPED WALNUTS (ABOUT 1 CUP)

**1** Preheat oven to 350°F.

**2** In a medium bowl combine flour, soda, baking powder, cloves, cinnamon, salt, and oats. Mix well with a wire whisk and set aside.

**3** In a large bowl with an electric mixer, blend sugars. Add butter and mix to form a grainy paste. Scrape down the sides of bowl.

**4** Add eggs and vanilla, and beat at medium speed until light and fluffy. Add carrots, pineapple, and nuts, and blend until combined. Batter will appear lumpy.

**5** Add flour mixture and blend at low speed until just combined. Do not overmix.

**6** Drop by rounded teaspoons onto ungreased cookie sheets, 1½ inches apart. Bake for 13 to 15 minutes, taking care not to brown cookies. Immediately transfer cookies with a spatula to a cool, flat surface.

# Creamy Lemon Macadamia Cookies

**Yield: About 2½ dozen**

| | |
|---|---|
| **2** | CUPS ALL-PURPOSE FLOUR |
| **½** | TEASPOON BAKING SODA |
| **¼** | TEASPOON SALT |
| **1** | CUP (PACKED) LIGHT BROWN SUGAR |
| **½** | CUP GRANULATED SUGAR |
| **1** | STICK (½ CUP) SALTED BUTTER, SOFTENED |
| **4** | OUNCES CREAM CHEESE, SOFTENED |
| **1** | LARGE EGG |
| **2** | TEASPOONS LEMON EXTRACT |
| **7** | OUNCES WHOLE MACADAMIA NUTS (ABOUT 1½ CUPS) |

**1** Preheat oven to 300°F.

**2** In a medium bowl, combine flour, soda, and salt. Mix well with wire whisk. Set aside.

**3** In a large bowl, blend sugars well with an electric mixer set at medium speed. Add the butter and cream cheese, and mix to form a smooth paste. Add the egg and lemon extract, and beat at medium speed until fully combined. Scrape down sides of bowl occasionally.

**4** Add the flour mixture and macadamia nuts. Blend at low speed just until combined. Do not overmix.

**5** Drop by rounded tablespoons onto ungreased cookie sheets, 2 inches apart. Bake for 18 to 20 minutes. Immediately transfer cookies with a spatula to a cool, flat surface.

# Peanut Butter Oatmeal Ranch Cookies

**Yield: About 3 dozen**

| | |
|---|---|
| **¾** | CUP WHOLE-WHEAT FLOUR |
| **¾** | CUP ALL-PURPOSE FLOUR |
| **½** | TEASPOON BAKING POWDER |
| **1** | CUP OATS (OLD FASHIONED OR QUICK) |
| **1** | CUP (PACKED) LIGHT BROWN SUGAR |
| **1** | STICK (½ CUP) SALTED BUTTER, SOFTENED |
| **½** | CUP CREAMY PEANUT BUTTER |
| **¼** | CUP HONEY |
| **2** | LARGE EGGS |
| **2** | TEASPOONS VANILLA EXTRACT |
| **6** | OUNCES RAISINS (ABOUT 1 CUP) |
| **3** | OUNCES SUNFLOWER SEEDS (ABOUT ½ CUP) |

**1** Preheat oven to 300°F.

**2** In a medium bowl, combine flours, baking powder, and oats. Mix well with a wire whisk and set aside.

**3** In a large bowl, beat sugar and butter with an electric mixer at medium speed to form a grainy paste. Blend together the peanut butter, honey, eggs, and vanilla. Scrape down sides of bowl.

**4** Add the flour mixture, raisins, and sunflower seeds. Blend at low speed just until combined. Do not overmix.

**5** Drop by rounded tablespoons onto ungreased cookie sheets, 2 inches apart. Bake for 18 to 22 minutes until bottoms turn golden brown. Immediately transfer cookies with a spatula to a cool, flat surface.

# Banana Nut Cookies

**Yield: About 4 dozen**

**2⅔** CUPS ALL-PURPOSE FLOUR
**½** TEASPOON BAKING SODA
**¼** TEASPOON SALT
**1** CUP (PACKED) LIGHT BROWN SUGAR
**½** CUP GRANULATED SUGAR
**2** STICKS (1 CUP) SALTED BUTTER, SOFTENED
**1** LARGE EGG
**1** TEASPOON CRÈME DE BANANES LIQUEUR OR BANANA EXTRACT
**¾** CUP MASHED RIPE BANANA (1 MEDIUM BANANA)
**12** OUNCES SEMISWEET CHOCOLATE CHIPS (ABOUT 2 CUPS)
**4** OUNCES CHOPPED WALNUTS (ABOUT 1 CUP)

**1** Preheat oven to 300°F.

**2** In medium bowl, combine flour, soda, and salt. Mix well with a wire whisk. Set aside.

**3** In large bowl with an electric mixer blend sugars at medium speed. Add butter and mix to form a grainy paste, scraping down the sides of the bowl. Add egg, liqueur, and banana, and beat at medium speed until smooth.

**4** Add the flour mixture, 1 cup of the chocolate chips, and the walnuts, and blend at low speed until just combined. Do not overmix.

**5** Drop by rounded tablespoons onto ungreased cookie sheets, 2 inches apart. Sprinkle cookies with chocolate chips, 6 to 8 per cookie. Bake for 20 to 24 minutes or until cookie edges begin to brown. Transfer immediately to a cool surface with a spatula.

# Chocolate Mint Cookies

**Yield: About 3 dozen**

**2⅔** CUPS ALL-PURPOSE FLOUR
**½** TEASPOON BAKING SODA
**¼** TEASPOON SALT
**½** CUP UNSWEETENED COCOA POWDER
**¾** CUP (PACKED) LIGHT BROWN SUGAR
**⅔** CUP GRANULATED SUGAR
**2** STICKS (1 CUP) SALTED BUTTER, SOFTENED
**3** LARGE EGGS
**1** TEASPOON MINT EXTRACT
**10** OUNCES MINT CHOCOLATE CHIPS (ABOUT 1¾ CUPS)

**1** Preheat oven to 300°F.

**2** In a medium bowl, combine flour, soda, salt, and cocoa powder. Mix well with a wire whisk and set aside.

**3** In a large bowl, blend sugars with an electric mixer at medium speed. Add butter and beat to form a grainy paste. Scrape sides of bowl, then add eggs and mint extract. Beat at medium speed until light and fluffy.

**4** Add the flour mixture and chocolate chips, and blend at low speed just until combined. Do not overmix.

**5** Drop dough by rounded tablespoons onto ungreased cookie sheets, 1½ inches apart. Bake for 19 to 21 minutes. Immediately transfer cookies with a spatula to a cool, flat surface.

# Fruitcake Cookies

**Yield: About 4½ dozen**

2   CUPS ALL-PURPOSE FLOUR
½   TEASPOON BAKING POWDER
1   CUP QUICK OATS (NOT INSTANT)
2   STICKS (1 CUP) SALTED BUTTER, SOFTENED
1½  CUPS (PACKED) LIGHT BROWN SUGAR
¼   CUP UNSULFURIZED MOLASSES
2   TEASPOONS BRANDY
2   TEASPOONS VANILLA EXTRACT
2   TEASPOONS ALMOND EXTRACT
2   LARGE EGGS
3   OUNCES RAISINS (ABOUT ½ CUP)
4   OUNCES CHOPPED PECANS (ABOUT 1 CUP)
2   OUNCES CHOPPED ALMONDS (ABOUT ½ CUP)
13½ OUNCES CANDIED CHERRIES, CHOPPED
    (ABOUT 2 CUPS)

## PREPARATION TIP
These cookies are fruitcake made easy. You just blend everything in your mixer—first the dry ingredients, then the wet, and finally the fruit pieces. A hand mixer or a stand-up mixer both work fine.

**1** Preheat oven to 300°F.

**2** In a medium bowl, combine flour, baking powder, and oats. Mix well with a wire whisk and set aside.

**3** In a large bowl, cream butter and sugar with an electric mixer at medium speed. Mix to form a grainy paste. Add molasses, brandy, almond and vanilla extracts and eggs; beat until smooth.

**4** Add flour mixture, raisins, pecans, almonds, and cherries. Blend at low speed just until combined. Do not overmix.

**5** Drop by rounded tablespoons onto ungreased cookie sheets, 1½ inches apart. Bake for 22 to 24 minutes or until cookies are set.

**6** Let cookies set on sheets for a few minutes, then transfer to a cool, flat surface. Top each cookie with a candied cherry half.

# Lacy Oatmeal Cookies

**Yield: About 8 dozen**

**1** CUP QUICK OATS (NOT INSTANT)
**¼** CUP ALL-PURPOSE FLOUR
**½** TEASPOON SALT
**1½** TEASPOONS BAKING POWDER
**1** CUP GRANULATED SUGAR
**1** STICK (½ CUP) SALTED BUTTER, SOFTENED
**1** LARGE EGG
**1** TEASPOON VANILLA EXTRACT

**1** Preheat oven to 325°F. Cover cookie sheets with foil, then coat with nonstick vegetable spray.

**2** In a medium bowl, combine oats, flour, salt, and baking powder. Mix well with a wire whisk and set aside.

**3** In a large bowl, combine sugar and butter with an electric mixer at medium speed to form a grainy paste. Add egg and vanilla, and beat until smooth. Add flour mixture and blend just until combined.

**4** Drop dough by teaspoons onto cookie sheets, 2½ inches apart. Bake for 9 to 12 minutes or until edges begin to turn golden brown. Let cool, then peel off cookies with your fingers.

**5** Be sure to respray the cookie sheets between batches.

# Choc-Co-Chunks

**Yield: About 3 dozen**

**2¼** CUPS ALL-PURPOSE FLOUR
**1** TEASPOON BAKING SODA
**1½** STICKS (¾ CUP) UNSALTED BUTTER, SOFTENED
**1** CUP (PACKED) DARK BROWN SUGAR
**2** LARGE EGGS
**2** TEASPOONS VANILLA EXTRACT
**1⅓** CUPS SHREDDED COCONUT
**12** OUNCES WHITE CHOCOLATE, CUT INTO CHUNKS
**1** CUP COARSELY CHOPPED MACADAMIA NUTS

**1** Preheat the oven to 300°F.

**2** In a small bowl, combine the flour and baking soda.

**3** In a medium bowl with an electric mixer, cream the butter and sugar. Beat in the eggs and vanilla. Beat in the flour mixture; do not overmix. Stir in the coconut, white chocolate chunks, and macadamia nuts.

**4** Drop the dough by rounded tablespoons 2 inches apart onto an ungreased cookie sheet. Bake for 18 to 20 minutes. Transfer to a wire rack to cool.

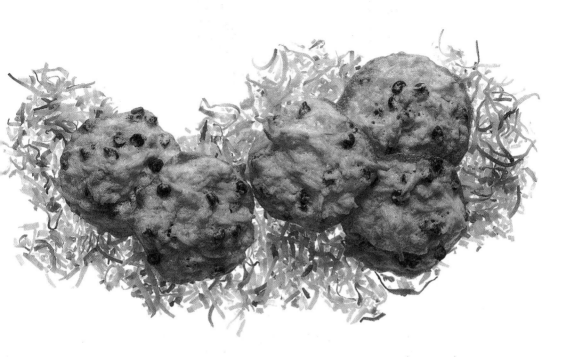

# Choconut Macaroons

**Yield: About 1½ dozen**

| | |
|---|---|
| ¼ | CUP GRANULATED SUGAR |
| 2 | TABLESPOONS ALMOND PASTE (MARZIPAN) |
| 1 | CUP SHREDDED SWEETENED COCONUT |
| 2 | OUNCES MINI SEMISWEET CHOCOLATE CHIPS (ABOUT ⅓ CUP) |
| 3 | LARGE EGG WHITES |
| ½ | TEASPOON CREAM OF TARTAR |

**1** Preheat oven to 325°F.

**2** Combine almond paste and sugar in a medium bowl. Using your fingers, work paste into sugar completely. Add coconut and chocolate chips and stir to combine.

**3** In another medium bowl, beat egg whites until fluffy using absolutely clean beaters. Add cream of tartar and beat on high until stiff peaks form. Add half of beaten egg whites to coconut mixture and combine to lighten. Fold in remaining whites gently, being careful not to deflate.

**4** Drop by rounded teaspoons onto lightly greased cookie sheets. Bake for 20 minutes, or until tops are lightly browned. Cool 1 minute on the cookie sheets before transferring cookies to a cool surface.

# FORMED AND FILLED COOKIES

## Almond Crunch Cookies

**Yield: About 1½ dozen**

| | |
|---|---|
| **1** | STICK (½ CUP) SALTED BUTTER, SOFTENED |
| **¾** | CUP GRANULATED SUGAR |
| **1** | LARGE EGG |
| **½** | TEASPOON ALMOND EXTRACT |
| **1** | OUNCE ALMONDS, GROUND IN BLENDER OR FOOD PROCESSOR (ABOUT ¼ CUP) |
| **4** | OUNCES SLICED ALMONDS (ABOUT 1 CUP) |
| **1** | CUP ALL-PURPOSE FLOUR |
| **¼** | CUP HEAVY CREAM |
| **6** | OUNCES SEMISWEET CHOCOLATE CHIPS (ABOUT 1 CUP) |
| **2** | TEASPOONS LIGHT CORN SYRUP |

**1** Preheat oven to 350°F.

**2** In a medium bowl, blend butter and sugar with an electric mixer until mixture forms a grainy paste. Scrape down sides of bowl, then add egg and almond extract. Beat at medium speed until light and fluffy.

**3** Add the ground almonds and flour, and blend at low speed just until combined. Do not overmix. Form dough into 1½-inch balls and roll in sliced almonds, coating each ball thoroughly.

**4** Place balls on ungreased cookie sheets, 2 inches apart. Bake for 15 to 18 minutes or until cookies are slightly brown along edges. Immediately transfer cookies to a cool surface covered with wax paper.

**5** Make the chocolate glaze: Scald cream in a small saucepan, then remove from heat. Stir in chocolate chips and corn syrup; cover and let stand for 15 minutes. With small wire whisk or wooden spoon, gently mix glaze until smooth, being careful not to create bubbles in the chocolate.

**6** When cookies are completely cool, drizzle patterns on them with the warm chocolate glaze, or dip half of each cookie into the glaze. Refrigerate the cookies on the wax paper until the glaze has set—about 10 minutes.

### PREPARATION TIP
Roll dough lightly between your hands into 1½-inch balls. The less you handle these cookies the lighter they will be. Then roll each ball in sliced almonds until fully coated.

# Chocolate-Glazed Shortbread Cookies

**Yield: About 4 dozen**

### Shortbread
**3**   STICKS (1½ CUPS) SALTED BUTTER, SOFTENED
**1**   CUP POWDERED SUGAR
**1**   TABLESPOON VANILLA EXTRACT
**3**   CUPS ALL-PURPOSE FLOUR

### Chocolate Glaze
**¼**   CUP HEAVY CREAM
**6**   OUNCES SEMISWEET CHOCOLATE CHIPS
       (ABOUT 1 CUP)
**2**   TEASPOONS LIGHT CORN SYRUP

**1** Preheat oven to 325°F.

**2** Blend butter until smooth in a large bowl using an electric mixer set at medium speed. Slowly blend in the powdered sugar. Scrape down the sides of the bowl, then add vanilla extract and combine thoroughly. Add flour and mix at low speed until well blended.

**3** Divide dough into 2 roughly equal pieces. Flatten each piece into a disk and wrap in plastic wrap. Refrigerate disks until firm, about 1½ hours.

**4** On a floured board using a floured rolling pin, roll out disks to ⅛-inch thickness. Turn dough often to prevent sticking. Cut cookies with flour-dipped cookie cutters. Bake on ungreased cookie sheets for 16 to 18 minutes, being careful not to let the cookies brown. Transfer cookies at once to a cool, flat surface with a spatula.

**5** Prepare the chocolate glaze: Heat cream in a small saucepan until scalded; remove from heat. Stir in chocolate chips and corn syrup, cover, and let stand for 15 minutes. With small wire whisk or wooden spoon gently mix glaze until smooth, being careful not to create bubbles in the chocolate. Dip all or half of each cookie into glaze and transfer to a tray or cool cookie sheet covered with wax paper. Chill cookies in refrigerator for 10 minutes to set.

# Russian Tea Cakes

Yield: About 2 dozen

## Cookies

**2**  STICKS (1 CUP) SALTED BUTTER, SOFTENED
**½**  CUP POWDERED SUGAR
**2**  TEASPOONS VANILLA EXTRACT
**2**  CUPS ALL-PURPOSE FLOUR
**¼**  TEASPOON SALT

## Topping

**½**  CUP FRUIT PRESERVES OR 2 OUNCES CHOPPED
WALNUTS (ABOUT ½ CUP)
**¼**  CUP POWDERED SUGAR


**1**  Preheat oven to 325°F.

**2**  In a large bowl, cream butter and sugar using an electric mixer. Add vanilla, scraping down sides of bowl as needed. Blend in flour and salt, mixing until thoroughly combined.

**3**  Roll tablespoons of dough into small balls about 1 inch in diameter. Place dough balls on lightly greased cookie sheets about 1 inch apart. Press down the center of each ball with a spoon, forming a depression. Fill each with a teaspoon of preserves or nuts.

**4**  Bake for 15 to 20 minutes or until golden brown. Transfer cookies immediately to a cool, flat surface. When cookies are completely cool, dust them lightly with powdered sugar.

# Gingersnaps

Yield: About 2½ dozen

**2½**  CUPS ALL-PURPOSE FLOUR
**½**  TEASPOON BAKING SODA
**¼**  TEASPOON SALT
**2**  TEASPOONS GROUND GINGER
**1**  TEASPOON DICED CRYSTALLIZED GINGER
**½**  TEASPOON ALLSPICE
**½**  TEASPOON GROUND BLACK PEPPER
**1¼**  CUPS (PACKED) DARK BROWN SUGAR
**1½**  STICKS (¾ CUP) SALTED BUTTER, SOFTENED
**1**  LARGE EGG
**¼**  CUP UNSULFURIZED MOLASSES


**1**  Preheat oven to 300°F.

**2**  In a medium bowl, combine flour, soda, salt, ground ginger, crystallized ginger, allspice, and pepper. Mix well with a wire whisk. Set aside.

**3**  In a large bowl, mix sugar and butter with an electric mixer set at medium speed. Scrape down the sides of the bowl. Add egg and molasses, and beat at medium speed until light and fluffy.

**4**  Add the flour mixture and mix at low speed just until combined. Do not overmix. Chill the dough in the refrigerator for 1 hour—the dough will be less sticky and easier to handle.

**5**  Form dough into balls 1 inch in diameter. Place onto ungreased cookie sheets, 1½ inches apart. Bake for 24 to 25 minutes. Use a spatula to immediately transfer cookies to a cool, flat surface.

# Chocolate Dreams

**Yield: About 2 ½ dozen**

## Cookies

**1½** STICKS (¾ CUP) SALTED BUTTER, SOFTENED
**½** CUP POWDERED SUGAR
**¼** CUP (PACKED) LIGHT BROWN SUGAR
**2** LARGE EGG YOLKS
**1** TEASPOON VANILLA EXTRACT
**1½** CUPS ALL-PURPOSE FLOUR

## Chocolate Filling

**½** CUP HEAVY CREAM
**6** OUNCES SEMISWEET CHOCOLATE CHIPS
(ABOUT 1 CUP)

## Topping

**2** TABLESPOONS GRANULATED SUGAR

**1** In a medium bowl, cream butter using an electric mixer set at medium speed. Add powdered and brown sugars and beat until smooth. Add yolks and vanilla, and mix at medium speed until light and fluffy. Scrape bowl. Add the flour and blend at low speed until thoroughly combined.

**2** Gather dough into a ball and flatten into a disk. Wrap dough tightly in plastic wrap or place in plastic bag. Refrigerate for 1 hour.

**3** Prepare the filling: Scald the cream in a small saucepan over medium heat. Add the chocolate chips and stir until melted. Remove from the heat.

**4** Preheat oven to 325°F.

**5** Using a floured rolling pin, roll dough on floured board to ¼-inch thickness. Cut circles with a 2-inch-diameter cookie cutter and place on ungreased cookie sheets, 1 inch apart. Continue using dough scraps, rerolling and cutting until all dough is used. Drop 1 teaspoon of chocolate filling in center of each circle and top with another circle. Completely seal the edges using the tines of a fork. Bake for 15 to 16 minutes, or until cookies are golden brown. Transfer cookies to a cool, flat surface with a metal spatula. Sprinkle with granulated sugar.

# Molasses Raisin Cookies

**Yield: About 4 dozen**

## Cookies

| | |
|---|---|
| **3 ¼** | CUPS ALL-PURPOSE FLOUR |
| **1** | TEASPOON BAKING SODA |
| **¼** | TEASPOON SALT |
| **2** | TEASPOONS GROUND CINNAMON |
| **1** | TEASPOON GROUND GINGER |
| **½** | TEASPOON ALLSPICE |
| **1** | CUP (PACKED) DARK BROWN SUGAR |
| **2** | STICKS (1 CUP) SALTED BUTTER, SOFTENED |
| **¾** | CUP UNSULFURIZED MOLASSES |
| **1** | LARGE EGG |
| **6** | OUNCES RAISINS (ABOUT 1½ CUPS) |

## Icing

| | |
|---|---|
| **1** | CUP POWDERED SUGAR |
| **2** | TABLESPOONS MILK |

**1** Preheat oven to 300°F.

**2** In a medium bowl, combine flour, soda, salt, cinnamon, ginger, and allspice. Mix well with a wire whisk and set aside.

**3** In a large bowl, beat sugar and butter with an electric mixer at medium speed until mixture forms a grainy paste. Scrape sides of bowl, then add molasses and egg. Beat until light and fluffy.

**4** Add the flour mixture and raisins, and blend at low speed just until combined. Do not overmix.

**5** Divide dough in half and shape each half into a roll 1½ inches in diameter. Wrap rolls in wax paper and refrigerate until firm, about 2 hours.

**6** Slice cookies ½ inch thick and place on ungreased cookie sheets, 1½ inches apart. Bake for 25 to 27 minutes until cookies are set.

**7** Immediately transfer cookies with a spatula to a cool surface.

**8** Prepare the icing: Blend sugar and milk in a small bowl until smooth. Using a small spoon or knife, drizzle cookies with icing.

## PREPARATION TIP
Unwrap the chilled rolls of dough and slice with a sharp knife into ½-inch-thick cookies. Place on ungreased cookie sheet.

# Cinnamon Maple Rings

**Yield: About 4 dozen**

## Pastry

| | |
|---|---|
| **2** | CUPS ALL-PURPOSE FLOUR |
| **¼** | CUP GRANULATED SUGAR |
| **2** | STICKS (1 CUP) SALTED BUTTER, CHILLED & SLICED INTO 8 PIECES |
| **¼** | CUP PURE MAPLE SYRUP, CHILLED |
| **2** | TO 4 TABLESPOONS ICE WATER |

## Filling

| | |
|---|---|
| **¼** | CUP GRANULATED SUGAR |
| **4** | TEASPOONS GROUND CINNAMON |

## Topping

| | |
|---|---|
| **¼** | CUP PURE MAPLE SYRUP |

**1** Combine flour and sugar in a medium bowl using an electric mixer set on medium speed. Add butter and mix until the dough forms pea-size pellets. Add chilled maple syrup and 2 tablespoons of water, and mix on low speed until dough can be formed into a ball. Do not overmix, or the pastry will be tough.

**2** Separate dough into 2 balls and flatten into disks. Wrap dough tightly in plastic wrap or place in plastic bags. Refrigerate for 2 hours or until firm.

**3** Prepare the filling: Combine sugar and cinnamon in a small bowl. Preheat oven to 325°F.

**4** Using a floured rolling pin on a floured board, roll one piece of dough into a rough rectangle 10 inches wide, 15 inches long, and ⅛ inch thick. Sprinkle dough with half of cinnamon-sugar filling. Starting with smaller side, roll dough up tightly into a cylinder. Dampen edge with water and seal. Repeat with remaining dough. Wrap each roll in plastic wrap and refrigerate for 1 hour.

**5** Using a sharp, thin knife, cut ¼-inch slices from each roll. Place slices on ungreased cookie sheets, 1 inch apart. Brush tops lightly with ¼ cup maple syrup. Bake for 16 to 17 minutes, or until light golden brown. Immediately transfer cookies to a cool, flat surface with a spatula.

## PREPARATION TIP

After sprinkling the dough with the cinnamon-sugar filling, roll the dough into a tight cylinder (*right*). Just before sliding the cookies into the oven, brush the tops with maple syrup (*far right*).

# Gingerbread Men

**Yield: About 2 ½ dozen 6-inch cookies
About 3 ½ dozen 4-inch cookies**

## Cookies

| | |
|---|---|
| **3 ¼** | CUPS ALL-PURPOSE FLOUR |
| **½** | TEASPOON BAKING SODA |
| **¼** | TEASPOON SALT |
| **1** | TEASPOON GROUND CINNAMON |
| **2** | TEASPOONS GROUND GINGER |
| **¼** | TEASPOON GROUND CLOVES |
| **2** | STICKS (1 CUP) SALTED BUTTER, SOFTENED |
| **¾** | CUP (PACKED) DARK BROWN SUGAR |
| **1** | LARGE EGG |
| **½** | CUP UNSULFURIZED MOLASSES |
| **3** | OUNCES RAISINS (ABOUT ½ CUP) (OPTIONAL) |

## Icing

| | |
|---|---|
| **⅔** | CUP POWDERED SUGAR |
| **1** | TO 2 TEASPOONS MILK |

**1** Preheat oven to 325°F.

**2** Combine flour, soda, salt, cinnamon, ginger, and cloves in a medium bowl.

**3** In a large bowl with an electric mixer cream butter and sugar. Scrape down the sides of the bowl. Add egg and molasses, and beat on medium speed until smooth. Scrape bowl and add the flour mixture. Blend on low speed just until combined; do not overmix.

**4** Separate dough into 2 balls and flatten into disks. Wrap each disk tightly in plastic wrap or a plastic bag, and refrigerate 1 hour or until firm.

**5** On floured surface with floured rolling pin, roll dough out to ¼-inch thickness. With floured cookie cutters, cut into gingerbread men. Gather scraps and reroll dough until all dough is used. Place on ungreased cookie sheets ½ inch apart.

**6** If you want to use raisins to decorate the cookies, plump raisins first by soaking them in warm water for 5 minutes. Discard water. Use raisins as eyes, mouths, and buttons.

**7** Bake for 9 to 11 minutes being careful not to brown. Transfer to a cool, flat surface with a spatula.

**8** Prepare the icing: Whisk sugar and milk together in a small bowl until mixture is smooth but liquid. If it seems dry, add ¼ teaspoon more milk. Spoon icing into a pastry bag fitted with a small piping tip. Decorate gingerbread men as desired.

# Brown Buttercrunch Cookies

**Yield: About 2 ½ dozen**

### Cookies
1    STICK (½ CUP) SALTED BUTTER, SOFTENED
½    CUP CORN SYRUP
⅔    CUP (PACKED) DARK BROWN SUGAR
1    CUP OLD-FASHIONED OATS
    (NOT QUICK OR INSTANT)
¾    CUP ALL-PURPOSE FLOUR
1    TEASPOON VANILLA EXTRACT

### Chocolate Glaze
¼    CUP HEAVY CREAM
6    OUNCES SEMISWEET CHOCOLATE CHIPS
    (ABOUT 1 CUP)
2    TEASPOONS LIGHT CORN SYRUP

**1**   Preheat oven to 375°F. Line cookie sheets with parchment paper.

**2**   In a medium saucepan, melt butter, corn syrup, and brown sugar over moderate heat, stirring constantly until sugar dissolves. Increase heat to high. When mixture boils remove from heat and stir in oats, flour, and vanilla.

**3**   Bake cookies 1 sheet at a time and be ready to work fast. Drop by half teaspoons 3 inches apart onto paper-lined cookie sheets. Bake for 8 minutes or until mixture spreads, bubbles, and begins to brown. Let cookies cool for 1 to 2 minutes before rolling.

**4**   Roll widest edge of cookie around a pencil or wooden spoon handle, creating a tube. Repeat with remaining cookies. If cookies become too brittle to roll, return to oven for about 30 seconds to soften. Cool rolled cookies completely.

**5**   Make the chocolate glaze: Heat cream in a small saucepan until scalded. Remove from heat and stir in chocolate chips and corn syrup. Cover and let stand about 15 minutes until chocolate has melted. Using a wire whisk or wooden spoon, gently mix the glaze until it is smooth, being careful not to create bubbles.

**6**   When cookies are cool, dip all or half of each cookie into the glaze and return to parchment paper. Refrigerate for 10 to 15 minutes to set.

# Brown Sugar Shortbread

**Yield: About 2 ½ dozen**

### Shortbread
**2** STICKS (1 CUP) SALTED BUTTER, SOFTENED
**¾** CUP (PACKED) LIGHT BROWN SUGAR
**2** TEASPOONS VANILLA EXTRACT
**2** CUPS ALL-PURPOSE FLOUR

### Topping
**1** TABLESPOON SALTED BUTTER
**6** OUNCES SEMISWEET CHOCOLATE CHIPS
(ABOUT 1 CUP)
**4** OUNCES PECANS, FINELY CHOPPED
(ABOUT 1 CUP)

**1** Preheat oven to 325°F.

**2** In a large bowl, cream butter and sugar with an electric mixer at medium speed. Scrape down sides of bowl. Then add vanilla and flour, and blend thoroughly on low speed.

**3** Shape level tablespoons of dough into 1-inch balls, then form into logs 2 inches long and 1 inch wide. Place on ungreased cookie sheets, 2 inches apart.

**4** Bake for 17 to 19 minutes, or until cookies spread, and turn a light golden brown. Transfer to a cool, flat surface.

**5** Make topping: Melt butter and chocolate chips in a double boiler over hot, not boiling, water, or in a microwave oven on high power. Stir chocolate every 30 seconds until melted.

**6** Dip top of each cooled shortbread cookie into melted chocolate, then into chopped pecans. Place cookies on wax paper and refrigerate to set.

# Fruit-Filled Jewels

**Yield: About 2 dozen**

**1½** STICKS (¾ CUP) SALTED BUTTER, SOFTENED
**½** CUP POWDERED SUGAR
**2** LARGE EGG YOLKS
**1** TEASPOON VANILLA EXTRACT
**1½** CUPS ALL-PURPOSE FLOUR
**1** CUP ANY FRUIT JAM

**1** Preheat oven to 325°F.

**2** In a medium bowl, cream butter with an electric mixer set at medium speed. Add sugar and beat until smooth. Add egg yolks and vanilla, and beat at medium speed until light and fluffy. Add the flour and blend at low speed until thoroughly combined.

**3** Gather dough into a ball and flatten into a disk. Wrap dough tightly in plastic wrap or place in plastic bag. Refrigerate for 1 hour.

**4** Using a floured rolling pin, roll dough on floured board to ¼-inch thickness. Cut circles with a 2-inch-diameter cookie cutter or drinking glass, and place on ungreased cookie sheets, 1 inch apart. Continue using dough scraps, rerolling and cutting until all the dough is used.

**5** Drop ½ teaspoon of fruit jam in center of each cookie, then top with another cookie. Using the tines of a fork, seal edges of cookies.

**6** Bake for 15 to 17 minutes or until edges begin to brown.

# Chocolate Cream-Filled Hearts

**Yield: About 2 ½ dozen**

### Cookies

**3** STICKS (1½ CUPS) SALTED BUTTER, SOFTENED
**1½** CUPS POWDERED SUGAR
**4** TEASPOONS VANILLA EXTRACT
**3** CUPS ALL-PURPOSE FLOUR

### Chocolate Cream Filling

**½** CUP HEAVY CREAM
**6** OUNCES SEMISWEET CHOCOLATE CHIPS
(ABOUT 1 CUP)

### Topping

**¼** CUP POWDERED SUGAR (OPTIONAL)

**1** Cream butter in a medium bowl with electric mixer set at medium speed. Add 1½ cups powdered sugar and beat until smooth. Add vanilla and mix until creamy. Scrape bowl. Add flour and mix at low speed until thoroughly mixed.

**2** Gather dough into 2 balls and flatten into disks. Wrap dough tightly in plastic wrap or place in an airtight plastic bag. Refrigerate for 1 hour or until firm.

**3** Preheat oven to 325°F.

**4** Using a floured rolling pin, roll dough on floured board to ¼-inch thickness. Cut out 2-inch hearts with cookie cutters. Continue using dough scraps, rerolling and recutting until all dough is used. Be careful not to overwork the dough.

**5** Place cookies on ungreased cookie sheets, ½ inch apart. Bake for 16 to 18 minutes or until firm. Transfer to cool, flat surface with spatula.

**6** Prepare the chocolate cream filling: Scald the cream in a small saucepan and remove from heat. Stir in the chocolate chips and cover for 15 minutes. Stir chocolate cream until smooth, then transfer to a small bowl. Set filling aside and let it cool to room temperature.

**7** Spread 1 teaspoon of chocolate filling on the bottom side of half of the cookies. Top with bottom side of another cookie, forming a sandwich. Repeat with remaining cookies and cream.

**8** If you wish, sift powdered sugar over the finished cookies.

## PREPARATION TIP
Spread the chocolate filling on the bottom side of one cookie heart.
Top with another heart, bottom side also touching the chocolate.

# Chocolate Sandwich Cookies

**Yield: About 1½ dozen**

## Cookies

| | |
|---|---|
| **1½** | STICKS (¾ CUP) SALTED BUTTER, SOFTENED |
| **¾** | CUP POWDERED SUGAR |
| **2** | TEASPOONS VANILLA EXTRACT |
| **¼** | CUP UNSWEETENED COCOA POWDER |
| **2** | TABLESPOONS CORNSTARCH |
| **1** | CUP ALL-PURPOSE FLOUR |

## Cream Filling

| | |
|---|---|
| **1** | STICK (½ CUP) SALTED BUTTER, SOFTENED |
| **1** | CUP POWDERED SUGAR |
| **2** | TEASPOONS VANILLA EXTRACT |
| **1** | TABLESPOON HEAVY CREAM |

**1** In a medium bowl, cream butter with an electric mixer at medium speed. Add sugar and beat until smooth. Add vanilla and beat at medium speed until light and fluffy. In another bowl, combine the cocoa, cornstarch, and flour, and mix well with a wire whisk. Add the cocoa mixture to the wet ingredients and mix at low speed until thoroughly combined.

**2** Gather dough into a ball and flatten into a disk. Wrap dough tightly in plastic wrap or place in an airtight plastic bag. Refrigerate for 1½ hours or until firm.

**3** Preheat oven to 325°F.

**4** Using a floured rolling pin, roll dough on floured board to ¼-inch thickness. Cut shapes with cookie cutters and place on ungreased cookie sheets, 1 inch apart. Continue using dough scraps, rerolling and cutting until all dough is used. Be careful not to overwork the dough. Bake for 16 to 18 minutes or until firm. Transfer cookies to a cool, flat surface with a spatula.

**5** Prepare the cream filling: Cream butter in a small bowl with an electric mixer set at medium speed. Add sugar, vanilla, and cream, and beat until smooth.

**6** Spread 1½ teaspoons of cream filling on the bottom sides of half of the cookies. Top with the remaining cookies.

# Surprise-Filled Cookies

**Yield: About 4 dozen**

**2½** CUPS ALL-PURPOSE FLOUR
**½** TEASPOON BAKING POWDER
**2** STICKS (1 CUP) SALTED BUTTER, SOFTENED
**1** CUP GRANULATED SUGAR
**1** LARGE EGG
**2** TEASPOONS VANILLA EXTRACT
**1** CUP FRUIT JAM

**1** Preheat oven to 300°F.

**2** In a medium bowl, combine flour and baking powder. Mix well with a wire whisk. Set aside.

**3** In another medium bowl with an electric mixer, cream butter and sugar. Add egg and vanilla, and beat on medium until smooth. Add the flour mixture and blend at low speed until thoroughly combined. Dough will be firm.

**4** Scoop tablespoonfuls of dough, roll into 1-inch-diameter balls, and place on ungreased cookie sheets, 1 inch apart. With the small end of a melon baller, scoop out the center of the dough balls. Do not scoop all the way through the cookie. Place ½ teaspoon of jam in the center of each dough ball. Place scooped-out dough back into mixing bowl to use to form more cookies.

**5** Bake for 22 to 24 minutes or until golden brown. Transfer to a cool, flat surface.

# Chocolate Peanut Florentines

**Yield: About 16 sandwich cookies**

**4** TABLESPOONS (¼ CUP) UNSALTED BUTTER
**¼** CUP (PACKED) LIGHT BROWN SUGAR
**¼** CUP LIGHT CORN SYRUP
**⅓** CUP ALL-PURPOSE FLOUR
**½** CUP FINELY CHOPPED UNSALTED PEANUTS
**1** TEASPOON VANILLA EXTRACT
**4** OUNCES SEMISWEET CHOCOLATE, FINELY CHOPPED

**1** Preheat the oven to 350°F. Butter and flour a cookie sheet.

**2** In a small saucepan, melt the butter over medium heat. Add the brown sugar and corn syrup and bring to a boil over medium heat, stirring constantly until the sugar dissolves, 3 to 5 minutes. Remove the pan from the heat and stir in the flour, peanuts, and vanilla.

**3** Quickly drop the batter in ½-teaspoon mounds 2 inches apart onto the prepared cookie sheet. Using a small spatula, spread each mound into an even circle.

**4** Bake for 9 to 10 minutes, or until browned; rotate the pan back to front halfway through the baking time. Cool on the cookie sheet for 1 to 2 minutes, then transfer to wire racks to cool completely.

**5** In a double boiler, melt the chocolate over hot, not simmering, water. Spread a thin layer of chocolate over the bottom (flat side) of one cookie. Cover with another cookie and gently press together. Repeat with the remaining cookies. Refrigerate the cookies to set the chocolate.

# Apple Cream Pennies

**Yield: About 6 dozen**

### Cookies

**2 ½** CUPS ALL-PURPOSE FLOUR
**½** TEASPOON BAKING SODA
**¼** TEASPOON SALT
**1** CUP (PACKED) DARK BROWN SUGAR
**½** CUP GRANULATED SUGAR
**2** STICKS (1 CUP) SALTED BUTTER, SOFTENED
**2** LARGE EGGS
**2** TEASPOONS VANILLA EXTRACT

### Filling

**8** OUNCES CREAM CHEESE, SOFTENED
**¼** CUP GRANULATED SUGAR
**¼** CUP APPLE BUTTER

**1** Preheat oven to 300°F.

**2** In a medium bowl, combine flour, soda, and salt. Mix well with a wire whisk. Set aside.

**3** Blend sugars in a large bowl using an electric mixer set at medium speed. Add butter and mix to form a grainy paste, scraping down the sides of the bowl. Add eggs and vanilla, and beat at medium speed until light and fluffy.

**4** Add the flour mixture and blend at low speed until just combined. Do not overmix.

**5** Shape dough into marble-size balls. Place balls on ungreased cookie sheets, 1 inch apart. Bake for 10 to 11 minutes. Do not brown. Transfer cookies to a cool, flat surface with a spatula.

**6** Prepare the filling: Blend cream cheese and sugar in a medium bowl with an electric mixer on medium until fluffy. Add apple butter and beat until filling is smooth and thoroughly combined.

**7** With a small knife spread 1 teaspoon of apple cream on the bottom half of each cooled cookie. Top with another cookie to create a sandwich. Repeat with remaining cookies and filling.

# Lemon Cream-Filled Cookies

**Yield: About 2 dozen**

### Cookies

**1½** STICKS (¾ CUP) SALTED BUTTER, SOFTENED
**½** CUP POWDERED SUGAR
**2** TEASPOONS LEMON EXTRACT
**1½** CUPS ALL-PURPOSE FLOUR
**¼** CUP CORNSTARCH

### Filling

**½** STICK (¼ CUP) SALTED BUTTER, SOFTENED
**1** CUP POWDERED SUGAR
**1** TABLESPOON HEAVY CREAM
 JUICE OF 1 FRESHLY SQUEEZED LEMON
 (ABOUT 2 TABLESPOONS)
 GRATED ZEST OF 1 LEMON (2 TO 3 TEASPOONS)

**1** Make the cookie dough: In a medium bowl, cream butter with an electric mixer set at medium speed. Add sugar and beat until smooth, scraping down sides of bowl as needed.

**2** Add lemon extract and beat until light and fluffy. Then add flour and cornstarch; blend at low speed until thoroughly combined.

**3** Gather dough into 2 balls of equal size and flatten into disks. Wrap the disks tightly in plastic wrap or a plastic bag. Refrigerate for 1 hour.

**4** Make the filling: In a small bowl, beat butter with mixer until fluffy. Gradually add sugar while continuing to beat. Add cream, lemon juice, and lemon zest. Mix until thoroughly blended and set aside. To harden filling quickly, refrigerate for 15 to 20 minutes.

**5** At this point, preheat the oven to 325°F.

**6** Using a floured rolling pin, roll the chilled cookie dough on a floured board to a ¼-inch thickness. Cut circles with a 2-inch-diameter cookie cutter or drinking glass. Place circles of dough on ungreased cookie sheets, ½ inch apart. Continue rolling out and cutting dough scraps until all dough is used.

**7** Bake for 15 to 17 minutes, or until edges begin to brown. Immediately transfer cookies with a spatula to a cool, flat surface.

**8** When cookies are completely cool, spread a cookie with 1 teaspoon of the lemon cream. Place another cookie on top of the filling to make a sandwich. Complete entire batch.

# Chocolate Glazed Creamy Lemon Turnovers

**Yield: 2 dozen turnovers**

## Pastry

| | |
|---|---|
| **2** | CUPS ALL-PURPOSE FLOUR |
| **2** | TABLESPOONS GRANULATED SUGAR |
| **½** | TEASPOON SALT |
| **1½** | STICKS (¾ CUP) COLD UNSALTED BUTTER, CUT INTO PIECES |
| **2** | OUNCES COLD CREAM CHEESE, CUT INTO PIECES |
| **3** | TABLESPOONS ICE WATER |

## Lemon Filling

| | |
|---|---|
| **6** | TABLESPOONS UNSALTED BUTTER |
| **4** | LARGE EGG YOLKS |
| **1** | LARGE EGG |
| **¾** | CUP GRANULATED SUGAR |
| **¼** | CUP FRESH LEMON JUICE |
| **2** | TEASPOONS GRATED LEMON PEEL |

## Toppings

| | |
|---|---|
| **1** | EGG, BEATEN |
| | GRANULATED SUGAR, FOR SPRINKLING |
| **5** | OUNCES SEMISWEET CHOCOLATE CHIPS |
| **½** | CUP HEAVY CREAM |

**1** Prepare the pastry: In a medium bowl, combine the flour, sugar, and salt. With a pastry blender, incorporate the butter and cream cheese until the mixture is the size of small peas. With a fork, stir in the ice water. Gather the dough into a ball, flatten into a disk, wrap in plastic, and chill in the refrigerator for about 30 minutes.

**2** Make the lemon filling: In a double boiler, melt the butter. In a medium bowl, whisk together the egg yolks, egg, sugar, lemon juice, and lemon peel. Add the egg mixture to the butter and cook, stirring frequently, until the mixture thickens and heavily coats the back of a spoon, about 15 minutes. Transfer the filling to a small bowl and refrigerate until firm, about 2 hours.

**3** Bake: Preheat the oven to 400°F. Cut the chilled dough in half and return half to the refrigerator. Roll the remaining half into a 12-by-16-inch rectangle. Cut into twelve 4-inch squares. Spoon about 1 tablespoon of filling into the center of each square. Moisten two adjacent sides of a pastry square with water, then fold the pastry over to form a triangle. Crimp the edges to seal. Brush each turnover with some of the beaten egg and cut three slits as steam vents. Sprinkle the tops with granulated sugar and place on an ungreased cookie sheet. Bake for 20 minutes, or until golden. Place on racks to cool to room temperature. Repeat with the remaining dough and filling.

**4** Meanwhile, make the chocolate glaze: Place the chocolate chips in a small bowl. In a small saucepan, bring the cream to a simmer. Pour the hot cream over the chocolate. Let stand, covered, for 5 minutes, then stir until smooth.

**5** Drizzle the turnovers with the chocolate glaze.

# Double-Dipped Chocolate Shortbread Cookies

**Yield: About 2 ½ dozen**

## Cookies

- **3** OUNCES SEMISWEET CHOCOLATE, FINELY CHOPPED
- **1½** STICKS (¾ CUP) UNSALTED BUTTER, SOFTENED
- **1** TEASPOON VANILLA EXTRACT
- **1½** CUPS ALL-PURPOSE FLOUR
- **½** CUP POWDERED SUGAR
- **2** TEASPOONS UNSWEETENED COCOA POWDER
- **⅛** TEASPOON SALT

## For Dipping

- **4** OUNCES WHITE CHOCOLATE, FINELY CHOPPED
- **½** CUP HEAVY CREAM
- **3** OUNCES SEMISWEET CHOCOLATE, FINELY CHOPPED

**1** Make the cookies: In a double boiler, melt the semisweet chocolate over hot, not simmering, water. Set aside to cool to lukewarm.

**2** In a large bowl with an electric mixer, cream the butter. Beat in the melted chocolate. Then beat in the vanilla, flour, sugar, cocoa, and salt. Wrap and chill the dough for 30 minutes, or until firm enough to roll into balls.

**3** Preheat the oven to 350°F. Roll the dough into 1-inch balls, then roll each ball into a thick log. Place on an ungreased cookie sheet and press the dough to a ¼-inch thickness with the tines of a fork, keeping the cookies oval in shape.

**4** Bake the cookies for 8 to 10 minutes, or until just set; do not overbake. Transfer to wire racks to cool completely.

**5** Dip the cookies: In a small bowl set over a saucepan of hot water, melt the white chocolate with ¼ cup of the cream; stir until smooth. Keep the mixture over the hot water so it will be liquid for dipping. In another small bowl set over a saucepan of hot water, melt the semisweet chocolate with the remaining ¼ cup cream; stir until smooth. Keep warm.

**6** Dip one end of a cookie in the white chocolate and the other end in the dark chocolate and return to the cooling racks so the chocolate can set. Repeat with the remaining cookies.

# Refrigerator Thumbprint Fudgy Cookies

**Yield: About 2½ dozen**

| | |
|---|---|
| ½ | STICK (¼ CUP) SALTED BUTTER, SOFTENED |
| ½ | CUP HEAVY CREAM |
| 1 | CUP GRANULATED SUGAR |
| 1 | TEASPOON VANILLA EXTRACT |
| 12 | OUNCES SEMISWEET CHOCOLATE CHIPS (ABOUT 2 CUPS) |
| 2½ | CUPS QUICK OATS (NOT INSTANT) |
| 1 | CUP RASPBERRY PRESERVES |
| ¼ | CUP POWDERED SUGAR |

**1** In a 2-quart saucepan, combine butter, cream, and sugar. Warm over medium heat, stirring constantly, until sugar dissolves. Remove from heat, add vanilla and chocolate chips, 1 cup at a time, stirring until chocolate melts. To complete the dough, fold in the oats and stir until all ingredients are thoroughly combined.

**2** Shape dough into 1-inch balls and place on a cookie sheet lined with wax paper. Using the bottom of a glass, flatten cookies to 2 inches in diameter. Make a depression in center of each cookie with your thumb. Chill cookies in refrigerator 30 minutes or until set. Spoon ½ teaspoon of preserves into center of each cookie. Dust with powdered sugar.

# Chocolate Chip Dough to Go

**Yield: About 4 dozen**

| | |
|---|---|
| 2 | CUPS ALL-PURPOSE FLOUR |
| 1 | CUP QUICK OATS (NOT INSTANT) |
| ½ | TEASPOON BAKING POWDER |
| ¼ | TEASPOON SALT |
| 2 | STICKS (1 CUP) UNSALTED BUTTER, SOFTENED |
| ¾ | CUP (PACKED) LIGHT BROWN SUGAR |
| ¾ | CUP GRANULATED SUGAR |
| 2 | LARGE EGGS |
| 2 | TEASPOONS VANILLA EXTRACT |
| 1 | CUP COARSELY CHOPPED PECANS |
| 12 | OUNCES SEMISWEET CHOCOLATE CHIPS (ABOUT 2 CUPS) |

**1** In a medium bowl, combine the flour, oats, baking powder, and salt. In another medium bowl with an electric mixer, cream the butter and sugars. Beat in the eggs and vanilla. Gently beat in the flour mixture; then stir in the pecans and chocolate chips.

**2** Turn half of the dough out onto a sheet of wax paper. Shape into a log 2 inches in diameter. Roll up the log of dough in the wax paper and twist the ends closed. Repeat with the remaining dough. Chill until firm. The cookie dough can be refrigerated for 1 week or frozen for 6 months stored in an airtight plastic bag.

**3** To bake the cookies, preheat the oven to 300°F. If using frozen dough, let it soften slightly at room temperature, then cut the dough log into ½-inch-thick slices. Place the slices on an ungreased cookie sheet 2 inches apart. Bake for 22 to 24 minutes, or until set.

# Pineapple Pocket Pies

**Yield: 32 pockets**

## Cookies

| | |
|---|---|
| **1** | CUP ALL-PURPOSE FLOUR |
| ½ | CUP WHOLE-WHEAT FLOUR |
| ½ | TEASPOON BAKING SODA |
| ½ | STICK (¼ CUP) SALTED BUTTER, SOFTENED |
| ¼ | CUP (PACKED) LIGHT BROWN SUGAR |
| ¼ | CUP HONEY |
| **1** | LARGE EGG |
| **1** | TEASPOON VANILLA EXTRACT |

## Filling

| | |
|---|---|
| ½ | CUP DRIED APRICOTS |
| ½ | CUP FRESH OR CANNED UNSWEETENED PINEAPPLE, IN CHUNKS |
| ¼ | CUP (PACKED) DARK BROWN SUGAR |
| **1½** | CUPS WATER |

**1** In a medium bowl, combine flours and soda. Mix well with a wire whisk. Set aside.

**2** In a large bowl with an electric mixer combine butter and sugar at medium speed. Add honey, egg, and vanilla and beat at medium speed until smooth. Scrape down the sides of the bowl, then add the flour mixture. Blend at low speed until just combined; do not overmix.

**3** Gather dough into a ball. Divide in half and roll into two 6-inch cylinders. Wrap each cylinder tightly in plastic wrap or in a plastic bag. Chill 1 hour.

**4** Prepare the filling: Combine all the filling ingredients in a medium saucepan over medium-low heat and stir until sugar dissolves. Turn heat up to medium and simmer—stirring occasionally—until mixture thickens and most of the liquid evaporates. Remove from heat and allow mixture to cool to room temperature. Purée filling in food processor or blender.

**5** Preheat oven to 325°F. Using your hands, roll each cylinder out to about 12 inches in length. Then place 1 cylinder on a floured board and using a floured rolling pin, roll into a rectangle roughly 5 inches wide, 18 inches long, and ⅛ inch thick.

**6** Spread half of the filling mixture down the center of the dough in a ribbon about 2 inches wide. With a metal spatula, loosen the dough, and fold each side lengthwise over the filling, one side overlapping the other by ½ inch.

**7** Cut strip in half widthwise. Use spatula to transfer each 9-inch strip onto an ungreased cookie sheet, turning the strips over so the seams are on the bottom. Repeat with remaining dough and filling.

**8** Bake for 20 to 22 minutes or until dough begins to turn a light gold. Do not brown. Cool strips on sheet for 1 minute, then transfer to a cool surface. When strips reach room temperature, cut each into 8 pieces with a thin, sharp knife.

# Jessica's Marshmallow Clouds

**Yield: About 3 ½ dozen**

**3**   CUPS ALL-PURPOSE FLOUR
**⅔**   CUP UNSWEETENED COCOA POWDER
**½**   TEASPOON BAKING SODA
**1**   CUP GRANULATED SUGAR
**1**   CUP (PACKED) LIGHT BROWN SUGAR
**2**   STICKS (1 CUP) SALTED BUTTER, SOFTENED
**2**   LARGE EGGS
**2**   TEASPOONS VANILLA EXTRACT
**12**  OUNCES MINI SEMISWEET CHOCOLATE CHIPS
    (ABOUT 2 CUPS)
**8**   OUNCES MINI MARSHMALLOWS, FROZEN

**1** Preheat oven to 350°F. Until you are ready to assemble the cookies just prior to baking, keep the marshmallows in the freezer—otherwise they will thaw too rapidly.

**2** In a medium bowl, combine flour, cocoa, and baking soda. Set aside.

**3** Combine sugars in a large bowl. Using an electric mixer, blend in butter, scraping down the sides of the bowl. Add eggs and vanilla, and beat at medium speed until light and fluffy.

**4** Add the flour mixture and chocolate chips, and blend at low speed until combined. Batter will be very stiff.

**5** Gather 4 or 5 frozen marshmallows in the palm of your hand and cover them with a heaping tablespoon of dough. Wrap the dough around the marshmallows, completely encasing them and forming a 2-inch-diameter dough ball.

**6** Place balls on ungreased cookie sheets, 2 inches apart. Bake for 10 to 12 minutes. Cool on sheet 2 minutes, then transfer to a cool, flat surface.

# Snowy White Chocolate Crescents

**Yield: About 2 ½ dozen**

**1 ½** CUPS ALL-PURPOSE FLOUR
**⅓** CUP COCOA POWDER, UNSWEETENED
**1** STICK (½ CUP) SALTED BUTTER, SOFTENED
**1** CUP GRANULATED SUGAR
**1** TEASPOON VANILLA EXTRACT
**1** LARGE EGG
**½** CUP POWDERED SUGAR

**1** Preheat oven to 325°F.

**2** In a small bowl, combine flour and cocoa. Mix well with a wire whisk and set aside.

**3** In a medium bowl, cream butter and sugar with an electric mixer on medium speed. Add vanilla and egg, and beat until light and smooth. Scrape down sides of bowl, then add flour and cocoa mixture. Blend on low speed until fully incorporated. The dough will be dry and crumbly.

**4** Shape a level tablespoon of dough into a 3 ½-inch log. Slightly bend the log to form a crescent shape. Form remaining dough into crescents, and place on ungreased cookie sheets, 1 inch apart. Bake for 15 to 17 minutes or until the outside of cookie is hard but the center remains soft.

**5** Cool on cookie sheets for 2 to 3 minutes, then transfer to a flat surface to cool a few minutes more. While still warm, roll the cookies in powdered sugar until coated.

# Glazed Honey-Nut Rolls

**Yield: About 20 nut rolls**

### Filling and Honey Glaze
¾    CUP CLOVER HONEY
⅓    CUP WATER
1    TEASPOON FRESH LEMON JUICE
1    CINNAMON STICK
8    OUNCES WALNUTS, COARSELY CHOPPED
4    OUNCES RAISINS (ABOUT ¾ CUP)
1    TEASPOON VANILLA EXTRACT
¼    TEASPOON ALMOND EXTRACT
6    OUNCES SEMISWEET CHOCOLATE CHIPS
    (ABOUT 1 CUP)

### Assembly
10   SHEETS (13 BY 22 INCHES) FROZEN PHYLLO
     DOUGH (ABOUT ¼ POUND), THAWED
1    STICK (½ CUP) UNSALTED BUTTER, MELTED

### Chocolate Glaze
⅓    CUP HEAVY CREAM
4    OUNCES SEMISWEET CHOCOLATE CHIPS
    POWDERED SUGAR, FOR DUSTING

**1** Prepare the filling: In a small saucepan, combine the honey, water, lemon juice, and cinnamon. Simmer for 10 minutes. Keep warm.

**2** In a medium bowl, combine the walnuts, raisins, vanilla, almond extract, and ½ cup of the honey mixture. Stir in the chocolate chips and set aside.

**3** Assemble and bake: Preheat the oven to 375°F. Keeping the rest of the phyllo covered with plastic wrap and a damp towel, lay a sheet of dough on a work surface. Cut in half crosswise. Brush each half with melted butter. With a short end facing you, spoon about 1½ tablespoons of filling onto the phyllo. Fold in the sides and roll up the dough. Brush the rolls with more butter and place on a cookie sheet. Repeat with the remaining dough, filling, and butter. Bake for 20 minutes, or until golden. Transfer to wire racks to cool, but immediately brush the rolls with the remaining honey glaze.

**4** Make the chocolate glaze: In a small saucepan, bring the cream to a simmer. Remove from the heat, add the chips, and let stand for 5 minutes; stir until smooth. Let cool, then drizzle over the nut rolls. Dust the rolls with powdered sugar.

# Linzer Cookies

**Yield: About 2 dozen**

## Cookies

| | |
|---|---|
| **1½** | CUPS ALL-PURPOSE FLOUR |
| **½** | CUP GROUND ALMONDS |
| **½** | TEASPOON BAKING POWDER |
| **¼** | TEASPOON SALT |
| **½** | TEASPOON GROUND CINNAMON |
| **1½** | STICKS (¾ CUP) SALTED BUTTER, SOFTENED |
| **¾** | CUP GRANULATED SUGAR |
| **2** | EGG YOLKS |
| **1** | TEASPOON VANILLA EXTRACT |
| **1** | TEASPOON ALMOND EXTRACT |

## Filling

| | |
|---|---|
| **½** | CUP RASPBERRY JAM |
| **1** | TEASPOON GRATED LEMON PEEL (½ OF 1 MEDIUM LEMON) |

## Topping

| | |
|---|---|
| **¼** | CUP POWDERED SUGAR |
| **2** | OUNCES SLICED ALMONDS (ABOUT ½ CUP) |

**1** Preheat oven to 300°F.

**2** Combine flour, almonds, baking powder, salt, and cinnamon with wire whisk.

**3** In a large bowl with an electric mixer cream butter and sugar. Add egg yolks and the vanilla and almond extracts, and beat at medium speed until light and fluffy. Add the flour mixture and blend at low speed until just combined. Do not overmix.

**4** Roll dough into 1½-inch balls. Place 2 inches apart on ungreased cookie sheets. With your index finger press an indentation in center of each ball to hold the filling.

**5** Bake for 22 to 24 minutes or until just golden brown on bottom. Transfer cookies to a cool, flat surface with a spatula.

**6** In a small bowl, combine jam and grated lemon peel. Sift powdered sugar over cookies. Place ½ teaspoon of filling mixture in center of cooled cookie and place sliced almonds in the jam filling.

# Chocolate Cashew Crunch

**Yield: About 3 dozen**

½  STICK (¼ CUP) UNSALTED BUTTER
⅓  CUP (PACKED) LIGHT BROWN SUGAR
¼  CUP LIGHT CORN SYRUP
½  CUP FINELY CHOPPED SALTED CASHEWS
⅓  CUP ALL-PURPOSE FLOUR
1½  TEASPOONS VANILLA EXTRACT
6  OUNCES MILK CHOCOLATE CHIPS
   (ABOUT 1 CUP)

**1**  Preheat the oven to 350°F. Butter and flour a cookie sheet.

**2**  In a small saucepan, melt the butter over medium heat. Add the brown sugar and corn syrup, then bring to a boil over medium heat, stirring constantly, until the sugar dissolves, 3 to 5 minutes. Remove from the heat.

**3**  Stir in the cashews, flour, and vanilla. Drop the batter in ½-teaspoon mounds 2 inches apart onto the prepared cookie sheet. Using a small spatula, spread each mound into a circle.

**4**  Bake for 8 to 10 minutes, or until browned, rotating the pan back to front after 4 minutes. Cool on the cookie sheet for about 30 seconds, then transfer to wire racks to cool completely.

**5**  In a small bowl set over a small saucepan, melt the chocolate over hot, not simmering, water. Dip the cookies halfway into the chocolate and return to the racks to set.

# Maple Pecan Butter Balls

**Yield: About 2 dozen**

1¼  CUPS ALL-PURPOSE FLOUR
½  TEASPOON BAKING SODA
1  TEASPOON GROUND CINNAMON
3  OUNCES PECANS, FINELY GROUND IN FOOD
   PROCESSOR OR BLENDER (ABOUT ¾ CUP)
1  STICK (½ CUP) SALTED BUTTER, SOFTENED
⅔  CUP GRANULATED SUGAR
¼  CUP PURE MAPLE SYRUP
1  LARGE EGG

**1**  Preheat oven to 300°F.

**2**  In a medium bowl, combine flour, soda, cinnamon, and finely ground pecans. (For extra flavor, sauté pecans in 1 tablespoon butter until slightly browned.) Mix ingredients well with a wire whisk and set aside.

**3**  In another medium bowl, cream butter and sugar with an electric mixer set at medium speed until mixture forms a grainy paste. Add syrup and egg and beat until slightly thickened.

**4**  Add the flour mixture and blend at low speed just until combined. Do not overmix. Place dough in a plastic bag and refrigerate until firm, about 1 hour.

**5**  Remove dough from refrigerator and shape into 1-inch balls. Place cookies on ungreased cookie sheets, 1 inch apart. Bake for 17 to 18 minutes, or until the cookie bottoms are golden brown. Immediately transfer the cookies with a spatula to a cool, flat surface.

> **PREPARATION TIP**
> To make cookies more festive, sprinkle them with powdered sugar using a small mesh sieve. Then, spoon chocolate icing into a pastry bag fitted with a small (#3) plain tip. Pipe decorative patterns onto cookies.

# BAR COOKIES

## Creamy Layered Pudding Bars

**Yield: 16 bars**

### Crust

| | |
|---|---|
| **1** | STICK (½ CUP) SALTED BUTTER, SOFTENED |
| **¼** | CUP GRANULATED SUGAR |
| **1** | LARGE EGG YOLK |
| **1** | TEASPOON VANILLA EXTRACT |
| **1** | CUP CAKE FLOUR |
| **⅛** | TEASPOON SALT |

### Filling

| | |
|---|---|
| **½** | CUP GRANULATED SUGAR |
| **1** | TABLESPOON CORNSTARCH |
| **5** | LARGE EGG YOLKS |
| **1** | TEASPOON VANILLA EXTRACT |
| **1** | CUP WHIPPING CREAM |
| **6** | OUNCES MINI SEMISWEET CHOCOLATE CHIPS (ABOUT 1 CUP) |
| **4** | OUNCES PECANS, CHOPPED (ABOUT 1 CUP) |

**PREPARATION TIP**
Press the chilled dough firmly into the bottom of a greased 8-by-8-inch pan. The dough should extend up the sides of the pan by about an inch. Lightly flour your hands before you begin to prevent the dough from sticking to them.

**1** Preheat oven to 325°F. Grease an 8-by-8-inch baking pan.

**2** In a medium bowl, cream the butter and sugar with an electric mixer at medium speed, scraping down the sides of the bowl. Add single egg yolk and vanilla and beat at medium speed until light and fluffy. Add the flour and the salt, and blend at low speed until just combined.

**3** Turn dough out into prepared pan, and place in refrigerator for 15 minutes. When dough is chilled, lightly flour your hands and press the dough to ¼-inch thickness on bottom and sides of pan. Dough should extend 1 inch up sides of pan. Return pan to refrigerator while you prepare the filling.

**4** Prepare the filling: Combine sugar and cornstarch in a small bowl. Mix well with a wire whisk. Set aside.

**5** In a medium bowl with an electric mixer set on medium-high speed, beat the 5 egg yolks 5 minutes or until they are light and fluffy. Add cornstarch-sugar mixture and mix on medium until combined. Add the vanilla, whipping cream, chocolate chips, and pecans and blend at low speed—scraping bowl as needed—until thoroughly combined. Pour filling into pastry-lined pan.

**6** Bake for 55 to 60 minutes or until filling is set and golden brown. Chill 4 hours or overnight. Cut into 16 bars.

# Vermont Maple Walnut Bars

**Yield: 12 to 16 bars**

## Bars

| | |
|---|---|
| **2** | CUPS ALL-PURPOSE FLOUR |
| ½ | TEASPOON BAKING SODA |
| ½ | CUP (PACKED) LIGHT BROWN SUGAR |
| **1** | STICK (½ CUP) SALTED BUTTER, SOFTENED |
| **1** | CUP PURE MAPLE SYRUP |
| **1** | LARGE EGG |
| **2** | TEASPOONS VANILLA EXTRACT |
| **4** | OUNCES WALNUTS, CHOPPED (ABOUT 1 CUP) |

## Maple Frosting

| | |
|---|---|
| **1** | STICK (½ CUP) SALTED BUTTER, SOFTENED |
| **2** | OUNCES CREAM CHEESE, SOFTENED |
| **1** | TABLESPOON (PACKED) LIGHT BROWN SUGAR |
| **3** | TABLESPOONS PURE MAPLE SYRUP |
| ¼ | CUP PLUS 2 TABLESPOONS POWDERED SUGAR |
| | WALNUT HALVES (OPTIONAL) |

**1** Preheat oven to 325°F. Grease an 8-by-8-inch baking pan.

**2** Make bars: In a medium bowl, combine flour and soda. Mix well with a wire whisk and set aside.

**3** In a large bowl with an electric mixer, blend sugar and butter to form a grainy paste. Scrape down sides of bowl, then add syrup, egg and vanilla. Beat at medium speed until smooth.

**4** Add the flour mixture and walnuts, and blend at low speed just until combined. Do not overmix.

**5** Pour batter into baking pan and smooth top with a spatula. Bake for 40 to 45 minutes or until toothpick inserted into center comes out clean. Cool in pan 15 minutes, then invert onto cooling rack. Cool completely before icing.

**6** Make frosting: In a medium bowl, cream butter and cream cheese with electric mixer at high speed. Add brown sugar and maple syrup, and beat until smooth. Reduce mixer speed to medium, and slowly add powdered sugar. Once sugar is incorporated, increase speed to high, and mix until smooth. If frosting appears thin, gradually add powdered sugar until frosting thickens.

**7** Using a metal spatula, spread frosting on top and sides of maple bars. If desired, make designs on frosting or decorate with walnut halves.

# Caramel-Filled Brownies

**Yield: 16 brownies**

## Brownies

**3** OUNCES UNSWEETENED CHOCOLATE
**1** STICK (½ CUP) SALTED BUTTER, SOFTENED
**4** LARGE EGGS
**1½** CUPS GRANULATED SUGAR
**1** TABLESPOON VANILLA EXTRACT
**1½** CUPS ALL-PURPOSE FLOUR

## Caramel

**½** STICK (¼ CUP) SALTED BUTTER
**⅓** CUP (PACKED) DARK BROWN SUGAR
**2** TABLESPOONS LIGHT CORN SYRUP
**1** TABLESPOON WHIPPING CREAM

**1** Preheat oven to 325°F. Grease an 8-by-8-inch baking pan.

**2** In a small saucepan, melt chocolate and ½ cup butter over low heat, stirring constantly. Remove from heat.

**3** Beat eggs in a large bowl using an electric mixer set on high speed until they thicken slightly. Add sugar slowly. Add vanilla and mix well. Add chocolate-butter mixture, and beat on medium until uniformly brown. Add the flour and blend at low speed until just combined. Do not overmix.

**4** Pour half of the brownie batter into the prepared pan. Smooth top. Bake for 15 to 20 minutes or until top is firm.

**5** Prepare the caramel: Heat butter, sugar, and corn syrup in heavy pan over medium heat, stirring constantly until sugar dissolves. Increase heat to high and boil 1½ minutes. Remove from heat and stir in cream. Keep warm.

**6** Spread warm caramel evenly over top of baked brownie layer. Pour remaining half of brownie mixture over caramel, smoothing the top. Bake an additional 25 to 30 minutes or until toothpick inserted into center comes cleanly out of top brownie layer. (Some caramel may stick to the toothpick.)

**7** Cool brownies in pan, then cut into squares. Serve at room temperature or chilled.

# Bull's Eyes

**Yield: 24 bars**

## Blue-Ribbon Chocolate Chip Cookies

**2½** CUPS ALL-PURPOSE FLOUR
**½** TEASPOON BAKING SODA
**¼** TEASPOON SALT
**1** CUP (PACKED) DARK BROWN SUGAR
**½** CUP GRANULATED SUGAR
**2** STICKS (1 CUP) SALTED BUTTER, SOFTENED
**2** LARGE EGGS
**2** TEASPOONS VANILLA EXTRACT
**12** OUNCES SEMISWEET CHOCOLATE CHIPS
(ABOUT 2 CUPS)
**1** CUP SWEETENED, SHREDDED COCONUT

## Double-Rich Chocolate Cookies

**1¼** CUPS ALL-PURPOSE FLOUR
**¼** TEASPOON BAKING SODA
**⅛** TEASPOON SALT
**¼** CUP UNSWEETENED COCOA POWDER
**½** CUP (PACKED) DARK BROWN SUGAR
**¼** CUP PLUS 2 TABLESPOONS
GRANULATED SUGAR
**1** STICK (½ CUP) SALTED BUTTER, SOFTENED
**1** LARGE EGG
**1** LARGE EGG YOLK
**1** TEASPOON VANILLA EXTRACT
**6** OUNCES SEMISWEET CHOCOLATE CHIPS
(ABOUT 1 CUP)

**1** Preheat oven to 300°F and grease a 9-by-13-inch glass baking dish.

**2** First, make the Blue-Ribbon Cookies: In a medium bowl combine flour, soda, and salt. Mix well.

**3** In a large bowl, blend sugars and butter with an electric mixer. Scrape sides of bowl, then add eggs and vanilla extract. Beat at medium speed until light and fluffy. Add flour mixture and chocolate chips, and mix just until combined. Press dough evenly into prepared pan and sprinkle with coconut. Set side.

**4** Next, make the Double-Rich Cookies: In a medium bowl combine flour, soda, salt, and cocoa powder with a wire whisk.

**5** In a large bowl, blend sugars and butter with mixer at medium speed. Scrape bowl, then add eggs and vanilla, and beat until well combined. Add the flour mixture and chocolate chips, and blend on low. Do not overmix.

**6** Drop the Double-Rich dough by rounded teaspoons onto the Blue-Ribbon dough. Evenly space the darker dough on top of the lighter dough to resemble bull's eyes. Bake 50 to 60 minutes, until a toothpick inserted in center comes out clean. Cool and cut.

# Twice-Topped Brownies

**Yield: 16 brownies**

### Brownie Layer

| | |
|---|---|
| **4** | OUNCES UNSWEETENED CHOCOLATE |
| **1** | STICK (½ CUP) SALTED BUTTER |
| **¾** | CUP ALL-PURPOSE FLOUR |
| **¼** | TEASPOON SALT |
| **2** | LARGE EGGS |
| **1** | CUP (PACKED) LIGHT BROWN SUGAR |
| **2** | TEASPOONS VANILLA EXTRACT |
| **½** | CUP CHOPPED PECANS |
| **½** | CUP MINI SEMISWEET CHOCOLATE CHIPS |

### Vanilla Cream

| | |
|---|---|
| **1** | STICK (½ CUP) SALTED BUTTER, SOFTENED |
| **4** | OUNCES CREAM CHEESE, SOFTENED |
| **1** | TEASPOON VANILLA EXTRACT |
| **1¼** | CUPS POWDERED SUGAR |

### Chocolate Drizzle

| | |
|---|---|
| **2** | OUNCES SEMISWEET CHOCOLATE CHIPS |
| **2** | TABLESPOONS HEAVY CREAM |

**1** Preheat the oven to 325°F. Grease a 7-by-11-inch baking pan.

**2** Prepare the brownie layer: In a double boiler, melt the unsweetened chocolate and butter together, stirring until smooth. Set aside to cool slightly.

**3** In a small bowl, combine the flour and salt.

**4** In a medium bowl, beat the eggs and brown sugar together. Beat in the chocolate mixture and the vanilla. Stir in the flour mixture. Then stir in the pecans and mini chocolate chips.

**5** Spread the batter in the prepared pan and bake for 22 to 25 minutes, or until a cake tester inserted into the center comes out clean. Cool in the pan on a rack.

**6** Make the vanilla cream: In a medium bowl, cream the butter and cream cheese until light and fluffy. Gradually beat in the vanilla and powdered sugar. Spread the vanilla cream over the cooled brownies. Refrigerate until set.

**7** Prepare the drizzle: In a double boiler, melt the chocolate chips and cream over hot, not simmering, water. Stir until smooth, then set aside to cool slightly. Dip a fork into the melted chocolate mixture and drizzle in a random pattern over the vanilla cream layer.

**8** Chill until ready to serve.

# Granola Date Bars

**Yield: 16 bars**

**Filling**

**8**  OUNCES CHOPPED DATES (ABOUT 1½ CUPS)
**½**  CUP SHREDDED SWEETENED COCONUT
**¾**  CUP HALF-AND-HALF OR LIGHT CREAM
**1**  TEASPOON VANILLA EXTRACT

**Granola Base**

**2**  CUPS QUICK OATS (NOT INSTANT)
**¾**  CUP ALL-PURPOSE FLOUR
**1**  CUP (PACKED) DARK BROWN SUGAR
**½**  TEASPOON BAKING SODA
**½**  TEASPOON GROUND CINNAMON
**1**  STICK (½ CUP) SALTED BUTTER, MELTED

**1** Prepare the filling: Heat dates, coconut, and half-and-half in a medium saucepan over medium heat. Stir occasionally until mixture boils and thickens, about 15 minutes. Remove from heat and stir in vanilla. Set aside to cool.

**2** Prepare the granola base: Combine oats, flour, sugar, soda, and cinnamon in a medium bowl. Mix well with wire whisk. Pour melted butter over dry ingredients and stir with large wooden spoon until thoroughly moistened.

**3** Press about 3 cups of the granola mixture into bottom of an 8-by-8-inch baking pan. Place in refrigerator for about 30 minutes to harden.

**4** Preheat oven to 350°F.

**5** Spread the cooled date filling evenly over the granola base. Sprinkle the remaining granola mixture (about ¾ cup) over the date filling. Bake for 25 to 30 minutes or until the granola topping is slightly browned and crisp. Cool to room temperature before cutting into 2-inch squares.

# Creamy Peanut Butter Chocolate Bars

**Yield: 24 to 36 bars**

## Crust

**8** MEDIUM-SIZE BUTTER OR CHOCOLATE CHIP COOKIES

**1** STICK (½ CUP) SALTED BUTTER, MELTED

## Chocolate Layers

**15** OUNCES MILK CHOCOLATE CHIPS (ABOUT 2½ CUPS)

## Peanut Butter Filling

**1½** CUPS CREAMY PEANUT BUTTER

**1** STICK (½ CUP) SALTED BUTTER, SOFTENED

**3** CUPS POWDERED SUGAR

**2** TEASPOONS VANILLA EXTRACT

**1** Preheat oven to 325°F.

**2** In food processor or blender, process cookies until finely ground. Add butter and mix together completely. Press crumb mixture into bottom of an 8-by-8-inch baking pan and bake for 10 minutes. Cool to room temperature.

**3** Melt chocolate in double boiler over slightly simmering water. Or microwave the chocolate, stirring every 30 seconds, until completely melted. Pour half of the melted chocolate into the pan and smooth evenly over crust. Place pan in refrigerator. Keep remaining chocolate warm.

**4** Prepare the peanut butter filling: Blend peanut butter and butter together until smooth using a food processor or an electric mixer. Slowly beat in powdered sugar and then add vanilla. Beat until smooth. Spread peanut butter filling over the chilled chocolate layer. Finish by pouring remaining warm chocolate over filling and spreading smooth. Chill in refrigerator for 1 hour or until firm. Cut into bars to serve.

### PREPARATION TIP

Spoon the peanut butter filling over the chilled chocolate and cookie base (*top*), then spread smooth. Complete the bar by pouring the melted chocolate over the peanut butter layer (*bottom*), spreading it smooth, and chilling in the refrigerator until firm.

# Golden White-Chunk Nutty Bars

**Yield: 16 bars**

| | |
|---|---|
| **2** | CUPS ALL-PURPOSE FLOUR |
| **½** | TEASPOON BAKING SODA |
| **¼** | TEASPOON SALT |
| **1½** | STICKS (¾ CUP) UNSALTED BUTTER, CUT INTO TABLESPOONS |
| **1** | CUP (PACKED) DARK BROWN SUGAR |
| **2** | LARGE EGGS |
| **½** | CUP SHREDDED COCONUT |
| **2** | TEASPOONS VANILLA EXTRACT |
| **10** | OUNCES WHITE CHOCOLATE, COARSELY CHOPPED |
| **1** | CUP COARSELY CHOPPED PECANS |

**1** Preheat the oven to 300°F. Grease a 9-by-13-inch baking pan.

**2** In a medium bowl, combine the flour, baking soda, and salt.

**3** In another medium bowl with an electric mixer, cream the butter and sugar. Beat in the eggs, coconut, and vanilla, then blend slowly until smooth. Add the flour mixture, chopped chocolate, and pecans.

**4** Scrape the dough into the prepared baking pan and level and smooth the surface. Bake for 40 to 45 minutes, or until the center is set and the top is golden.

**5** Place the pan on a wire rack to cool to room temperature before cutting into 16 bars.

# Pecan Pie Bars

**Yield: 16 bars**

**Pastry**

**1½** CUPS ALL-PURPOSE FLOUR
**1** STICK (½ CUP) SALTED BUTTER, CHILLED
**5** TO 6 TABLESPOONS ICE WATER

**Filling**

**5** TABLESPOONS SALTED BUTTER
**1** CUP (PACKED) DARK BROWN SUGAR
**½** CUP LIGHT CORN SYRUP
**2** TEASPOONS VANILLA EXTRACT
**3** LARGE EGGS, BEATEN
**6** OUNCES CHOPPED PECANS (ABOUT 1½ CUPS)
**16** PECAN HALVES

**1** Preheat oven to 350°F.

**2** In a medium bowl, combine flour and chilled butter with a pastry cutter until dough resembles course meal. Add water gradually and mix just until dough holds together and can be shaped into a ball. Or, use a food processor fitted with metal blade to combine flour and butter. Add water by tablespoonfuls and process just until a dough ball begins to form. Wrap dough tightly in plastic wrap or a plastic bag. Refrigerate for 1 hour or until firm.

**3** On floured board using a floured rolling pin, roll out dough into a 10-inch square. Fold dough in half and then into quarters. Place it in an 8-by-8-inch baking pan. Unfold the dough and press it into the corners and up along the sides of the pan. Refrigerate for 15 minutes.

**4** Prepare the filling: Melt 5 tablespoons of butter in a medium saucepan over medium heat. Remove from heat, and stir in sugar and corn syrup. Mix until smooth. Add vanilla and eggs, and beat with spoon until thoroughly combined. Fold in chopped pecans.

**5** Pour the pecan filling into the pastry-lined pan. If dough extends beyond filling mixture trim dough with a knife. Place pan in center of oven and bake 50 to 60 minutes or until filling is set. Cool on wire rack. Cut into 2-inch squares, and top with a pecan half. Serve chilled or at room temperature.

# Tuxedo Cookie Bars

**Yield: 18 bars**

**1½** CUPS ALL-PURPOSE FLOUR
**1** TEASPOON BAKING SODA
**1** STICK (½ CUP) SALTED BUTTER
**1½** CUPS GRANULATED SUGAR
**18** OUNCES SEMISWEET CHOCOLATE CHIPS (ABOUT 3 CUPS)
**1** TABLESPOON VANILLA EXTRACT
**4** TABLESPOONS HOT WATER
**4** LARGE EGGS
**6** OUNCES WHITE CHOCOLATE CHIPS (ABOUT 1 CUP)

**1** Preheat oven to 325°F. Grease a 9-by-13-inch baking pan.

**2** In a medium bowl, combine flour and soda with a wire whisk, and set aside.

**3** In a small saucepan, melt butter and 2 cups of the semisweet chips over low heat, stirring constantly until smooth.

**4** In a large bowl with an electric mixer at medium speed, beat chocolate mixture and sugar until smooth, about 5 minutes. Continuing to beat, add the vanilla, then the water, a tablespoon at a time. Scrape down sides of bowl. Next, add eggs one at a time, mixing well after each addition.

**5** Gradually add the flour mixture, blending at low speed. Then add the remaining 1 cup of semisweet chips and the white chocolate chips. Blend until equally distributed throughout the batter.

**6** Spread batter into prepared baking pan. Bake for 35 to 40 minutes or until toothpick inserted into center comes out just slightly moist.

**7** Cool to room temperature. Cover well and refrigerate until cold. Cut into bars to serve.

# Brownies Espresso

**Yield: 12 to 16 servings**

### Brownies

**2 ½** CUPS ALL-PURPOSE FLOUR
**½** TEASPOON BAKING SODA
**1** CUP (PACKED) DARK BROWN SUGAR
**½** CUP GRANULATED SUGAR
**2** STICKS (1 CUP) SALTED BUTTER, SOFTENED
**2** OUNCES UNSWEETENED BAKING CHOCOLATE
**1** TABLESPOON INSTANT ESPRESSO OR
    INSTANT COFFEE GRANULES
**1** TABLESPOON BOILING WATER
**2** LARGE EGGS
**1** TEASPOON VANILLA EXTRACT
**1** TEASPOON ALMOND EXTRACT
**1** CUP (6 OUNCES) SEMISWEET CHOCOLATE CHIPS

### Glaze

**3** OUNCES SEMISWEET CHOCOLATE
**⅓** CUP SALTED BUTTER, SOFTENED
**½** CUP SLICED ALMONDS

**1** Preheat oven to 325°F. Grease an 8-by-8-inch baking pan.

**2** In a medium bowl combine flour and soda. Mix well with a wire whisk and set aside.

**3** In a large bowl blend sugars with an electric mixer at medium speed. Add butter and mix to form a grainy paste.

**4** Melt baking chocolate in a double boiler. Meanwhile, in a small bowl, dissolve espresso or coffee granules in boiling water.

**5** Add chocolate and coffee to sugar and butter; beat at medium speed until smooth. Add eggs, vanilla and almond extracts; beat until smooth.

**6** Scrape down sides of bowl. Add the flour mixture and chocolate chips, and blend at low speed just until combined. Do not overmix.

**7** Pour batter into greased baking pan. Bake for 35 to 40 minutes or until toothpick placed in center comes out clean. Cool in pan for 15 minutes. Invert on rack.

**8** To make glaze: Melt together the chocolate and butter in a double boiler, stirring until smooth.

**9** Spread glaze over brownies and sprinkle with almonds. Cool completely before cutting into bars.

# Cherry Cream Bars

**Yield: 12 bars**

## Brownie Layer

| | |
|---|---|
| **1** | CUP ALL-PURPOSE FLOUR |
| **1** | CUP GRANULATED SUGAR |
| **¾** | CUP (PACKED) DARK BROWN SUGAR |
| **½** | TEASPOON SALT |
| **4** | OUNCES UNSWEETENED CHOCOLATE |
| **1½** | STICKS (¾ CUP) UNSALTED BUTTER, SOFTENED |
| **4** | LARGE EGGS |
| **¼** | CUP MILK |
| **2½** | TEASPOONS VANILLA EXTRACT |
| **1** | CUP COARSELY CHOPPED WALNUTS |
| **1** | CUP DRAINED CANNED BING CHERRIES (½ CUP OF THE SYRUP RESERVED) |
| **1** | CUP SEMISWEET CHOCOLATE CHIPS |

## Chocolate-Cherry Glaze

| | |
|---|---|
| **3** | OUNCES SEMISWEET CHOCOLATE, CHOPPED |
| **½** | CUP SYRUP RESERVED FROM CHERRIES |
| **¼** | CUP HEAVY CREAM |
| **2** | TEASPOONS KIRSCH (CHERRY BRANDY) |
| **2** | TEASPOONS GRANULATED SUGAR |

## Cherry Cream

| | |
|---|---|
| **1** | CUP HEAVY CREAM |
| **3** | TABLESPOONS POWDERED SUGAR |
| **1** | TABLESPOON KIRSCH (CHERRY BRANDY) |
| **½** | CUP CHOPPED DRAINED CANNED BING CHERRIES |

**1** Preheat the oven to 300°F. Grease a 7-by-11-inch baking pan.

**2** Make the brownie layer: In a large bowl, whisk together the flour, granulated sugar, brown sugar, and salt.

**3** In a double boiler, melt the unsweetened chocolate and butter together over low heat, stirring until smooth.

**4** In a small bowl, lightly beat the eggs with the milk and vanilla.

**5** Add the chocolate mixture and beaten eggs to the dry ingredients and stir to blend. Stir in the walnuts, cherries, and chocolate chips.

**6** Pour the batter into the prepared pan and bake for 1 hour and 10 minutes, or until a cake tester inserted in the center comes out with a few crumbs clinging to it. Cool the brownies in the pan on a rack.

**7** Meanwhile, make the chocolate-cherry glaze: Place the semisweet chocolate in a medium bowl.

**8** In a small saucepan, bring the reserved cherry syrup to a boil. Simmer until reduced by half. Add the cream and bring to a boil. Remove from the heat and stir in the kirsch and granulated sugar.

**9** Pour the hot cream mixture over the chocolate. Let stand, covered, for 5 minutes, then stir until smooth. Set aside to cool to room temperature, then pour the glaze over the cooled brownies.

**10** Make the cherry cream: In a medium bowl, beat the cream with the powdered sugar and kirsch until stiff peaks form. Fold in the drained chopped cherries.

**11** Cut into 12 bars and serve with a spoonful of the cherry cream on top.

# Kandy Fun Kakes

## Yield: 16 squares

| | |
|---|---|
| ½ | STICK (¼ CUP) UNSALTED BUTTER |
| 4 | CUPS MINI MARSHMALLOWS |
| 2 | TEASPOONS VANILLA EXTRACT |
| 4 | CUPS CRISP RICE CEREAL |
| ¾ | CUP BUTTERSCOTCH CARAMEL FUDGE TOPPING |
| 12 | OUNCES MILK CHOCOLATE, COARSELY CHOPPED |

**1** Lightly grease a 7-by-11-inch or an 8-by-8 inch baking pan.

**2** In a large saucepan, melt the butter over low heat. Add the marshmallows and stir until blended. Remove from the heat and stir in the vanilla.

**3** Stir in the cereal and mix with a wooden spoon until thoroughly blended. Scrape the mixture into the prepared pan. With lightly buttered hands or a lightly buttered spatula, press gently on the mixture to level. Place in the freezer for 10 minutes.

**4** In a small saucepan, warm the butterscotch caramel fudge topping to lukewarm (do not let it get hot). Remove from the heat and set aside to cool slightly.

**5** Pour the warm butterscotch topping over the cereal layer, spreading evenly. Place in the freezer for 10 minutes.

**6** In a double boiler, melt the chocolate over hot, not simmering, water. Set aside to cool slightly. Spread the chocolate on top of the caramel mixture. Chill to set the chocolate. Cut into squares and serve.

# Coconut Mud Bars

**Yield: 24 bars**

## Bottom Layer

**1⅓** CUPS ALL-PURPOSE FLOUR
**½** TEASPOON BAKING POWDER
PINCH OF SALT
**½** CUP (PACKED) DARK BROWN SUGAR
**1** STICK (½ CUP) UNSALTED BUTTER, SLIGHTLY SOFTENED AND CUT INTO SMALL PIECES

## Ganache

**10** OUNCES SEMISWEET CHOCOLATE, FINELY CHOPPED
**¾** CUP HEAVY CREAM

## Topping

**4** TABLESPOONS (¼ CUP) UNSALTED BUTTER, SOFTENED
**½** CUP GRANULATED SUGAR
**2** TEASPOONS VANILLA EXTRACT
**¼** TEASPOON COCONUT EXTRACT (OPTIONAL)
**2** LARGE EGGS
**1½** CUPS SHREDDED COCONUT
**1½** CUPS CHOPPED PECANS

**1** Preheat the oven to 350°F. Lightly grease a 9-by-13-inch baking pan.

**2** Make the bottom layer: In a medium bowl, combine the flour, baking powder, salt, and brown sugar. With a pastry blender, cut the butter into the dry ingredients until the mixture resembles coarse meal. Press the mixture into the bottom of the prepared pan. Bake for 10 minutes, or until the crust is just set. Place the pan on a rack to cool, but leave the oven on.

**3** Meanwhile, make the ganache: Place the chocolate in a medium bowl. In a small saucepan, bring the cream to a simmer. Pour the hot cream over the chocolate; let stand for 5 minutes, then stir until smooth. Pour the ganache over the crust and refrigerate for about 15 minutes to set the ganache.

**4** Prepare the topping: In a medium bowl, cream the butter. Add the granulated sugar, vanilla, and coconut extract, if desired, and beat until blended. Beat in the eggs. Stir in the coconut and pecans.

**5** Drop the coconut-pecan topping evenly over the ganache and spread gently. Bake for 25 to 30 minutes, or until the top is golden brown. Set the pan on a wire rack to cool. Cut into bars.

# Super Fudge Brownies

**Yield: 16 brownies, 2 inches square**

| | |
|---|---|
| **6** | OUNCES UNSWEETENED BAKING CHOCOLATE |
| **2** | STICKS (1 CUP) SALTED BUTTER, SOFTENED |
| **4** | LARGE EGGS |
| **2** | CUPS GRANULATED SUGAR |
| **1** | TABLESPOON VANILLA EXTRACT |
| **½** | CUP ALL-PURPOSE FLOUR |
| **6** | OUNCES SEMISWEET CHOCOLATE CHIPS (ABOUT 1 CUP) |

**1** Preheat oven to 300°F. Grease an 8-by-8-inch baking pan.

**2** Combine unsweetened baking chocolate and butter in a medium saucepan. Melt over medium-low heat, stirring constantly until pieces are almost melted. Remove from heat and stir until smooth.

**3** In a large bowl, using an electric mixer on medium speed, beat eggs until light yellow in color—about 5 minutes. Add sugar and blend on low until thoroughly combined.

**4** Add vanilla and melted chocolate to the egg and sugar mixture. Blend on low speed until smooth. Add the flour and mix thoroughly.

**5** Pour batter into greased pan. Smooth surface with a spatula, and sprinkle uniformly with chocolate chips. Bake on the center rack of oven for 45 to 55 minutes. The batter should be set and a toothpick inserted into the center should come out clean. Do not overbake.

**6** Cool to room temperature. Cover and refrigerate for at least 1 hour. Cut and serve chilled.

# Chocolate Chip Butterscotch Bars

**Yield: 16 bars**

**2**   CUPS ALL-PURPOSE FLOUR
**½**   TEASPOON BAKING SODA
**1**   CUP (PACKED) DARK BROWN SUGAR
**2**   STICKS (1 CUP) SALTED BUTTER, SOFTENED
**1**   LARGE EGG
**2**   TEASPOONS VANILLA EXTRACT
**4**   OUNCES CHOPPED PECANS (ABOUT 1 CUP)
**9**   OUNCES SEMISWEET CHOCOLATE CHIPS
    (ABOUT 1½ CUPS)

**1** Preheat oven to 300°F. Grease an 8-by-8-inch baking pan.

**2** Combine flour and soda in a medium bowl. Mix well with a wire whisk. Set aside.

**3** In a large bowl, use an electric mixer to blend the sugar and butter. Add egg and vanilla, and beat at medium speed until light and smooth. Scrape down the sides of the bowl, then add the flour mixture, pecans, and chocolate chips. Blend at low speed until just combined. Do not overmix.

**4** Transfer batter into the prepared pan, and level top with a rubber spatula. Bake in center of oven for 35 to 45 minutes or until toothpick comes out clean but center is still soft. Cool on rack to room temperature. Cut with sharp knife into 1-by-2-inch bars.

# Reduced-Fat Chocolate Brownies

**Yield: 16 brownies**

| | |
|---|---|
| ½ | CUP WATER |
| **3** | OUNCES PITTED PRUNES (ABOUT 9 PRUNES) |
| ¾ | CUP PLUS 1 TABLESPOON ALL-PURPOSE FLOUR |
| ½ | CUP UNSWEETENED COCOA POWDER |
| ½ | TEASPOON BAKING POWDER |
| ¼ | TEASPOON SALT |
| ½ | STICK (¼ CUP) UNSALTED BUTTER |
| **1** | CUP (PACKED) LIGHT BROWN SUGAR |
| ½ | CUP UNSWEETENED APPLESAUCE |
| **2** | TEASPOONS VANILLA EXTRACT |
| **4** | EGG WHITES |
| ¼ | CUP MINI SEMISWEET CHOCOLATE CHIPS (OPTIONAL) |

**1** Preheat the oven to 325°F. Spray an 8-by-8-inch baking pan with nonstick cooking spray.

**2** In a small, heavy saucepan, bring the water to a boil. Add the prunes, cover, reduce the heat, and simmer for 5 minutes. Remove from the heat and set aside to steep for 5 minutes. Uncover and let cool to room temperature. Drain the liquid and purée the prunes.

**3** In a small bowl, whisk together the flour, cocoa, baking powder, and salt.

**4** In a medium bowl with an electric mixer, cream the butter and sugar. Beat in the prune purée, applesauce, and vanilla. Beat in the egg whites. Beat in the flour mixture.

**5** Spread the batter in the prepared pan and smooth the top. Sprinkle with the chocolate chips, if desired. Bake for 35 to 40 minutes, or until the center springs back when lightly pressed; do not overbake.

**6** Cool in the pan on a rack, then cut into 16 squares.

# Peanut Butter and Jelly Squares

**Yield: 24 squares**

**2 ½** CUPS ALL-PURPOSE FLOUR
**½** TEASPOON BAKING POWDER
**2** STICKS (1 CUP) SALTED BUTTER, SOFTENED
**1** CUP GRANULATED SUGAR
**1** LARGE EGG
**2** TEASPOONS VANILLA EXTRACT
**½** CUP JAM OR JELLY
**¼** CUP CREAMY PEANUT BUTTER
**2** TABLESPOONS POWDERED SUGAR

**1** Preheat oven to 325°F. Lightly grease a 9-by-13-inch baking pan.

**2** In a medium bowl, combine flour and baking powder. Mix well with a wire whisk and set aside.

**3** In another medium bowl with an electric mixer on medium speed, combine butter and sugar to form a grainy paste. Add egg and vanilla, and mix until smooth. Scrape down sides of bowl. Then add flour mixture and blend at low speed until thoroughly combined. Dough will be firm.

**4** Divide dough into 2 pieces; form disks and wrap tightly in plastic wrap or a plastic bag. Refrigerate for 1 hour.

**5** On floured board using a floured rolling pin, roll out each disk to 9 by 13 inches, about ¼ inch thick. Place 1 piece in bottom and up the sides of prepared baking pan. Refrigerate 10 minutes more.

**6** Spread half the jelly on dough. Layer peanut butter on top of jelly, then top with remaining jelly. Sprinkle with powdered sugar. Place second dough rectangle on top of peanut-butter-and-jelly layer. Pinch down side edges all around inside of pan.

**7** Bake for 35 to 40 minutes or until golden brown and firm to the touch in the center. Cool in pan, then cut into squares.

# TARTS, CAKES, AND PIES

## Lemon-Glazed Pound Cake

**Yield: 2 dozen slices**

### Cake

| | |
|---|---|
| **3** | CUPS CAKE FLOUR, SIFTED |
| **2** | CUPS GRANULATED SUGAR |
| **½** | TEASPOON SALT |
| **1** | TEASPOON BAKING POWDER |
| **3** | STICKS (1½ CUPS) SALTED BUTTER, SOFTENED |
| **⅓** | CUP BUTTERMILK, AT ROOM TEMPERATURE |
| **6** | LARGE EGGS |
| **2** | TEASPOONS LEMON EXTRACT |
| **1** | TABLESPOON GRATED LEMON ZEST (2 MEDIUM LEMONS) |

### Glaze

| | |
|---|---|
| **¼** | CUP FRESHLY SQUEEZED LEMON JUICE |
| **¼** | CUP GRANULATED SUGAR |

### Topping

| | |
|---|---|
| **2** | TABLESPOONS POWDERED SUGAR, SIFTED |

**1** Preheat oven to 350°F. Grease and flour a 3-quart fluted tube pan or bundt pan.

**2** In a large bowl with an electric mixer on low speed, blend flour, sugar, salt and baking powder. Add butter, buttermilk and 3 eggs. Beat on low until dry ingredients are moistened. Increase speed to high and beat for 2 minutes. Scrape down sides of bowl.

**3** Add lemon extract and lemon zest, and blend at medium speed. Add the remaining 3 eggs one at a time, beating at high speed for 30 seconds after each addition.

**4** Pour batter into prepared pan, and bake for 50 to 60 minutes or until a toothpick inserted into cake comes out clean.

**5** While pound cake is baking, prepare lemon glaze. In a small saucepan heat lemon juice and sugar over low heat. Stir constantly until sugar dissolves.

**6** When cake is done, remove from oven and leave cake in pan. With a toothpick, poke holes in the surface of the cake, and pour half the glaze over it.

**7** Cool in pan 15 minutes, then invert on cooling rack. Brush top of pound cake with remaining lemon glaze. Cool to room temperature, then dust with powdered sugar.

### PREPARATION TIP

With a toothpick, poke holes in the surface of the cake. Then pour the lemon glaze over the holes, letting it drizzle into the cake. Saturating this pound cake with lemon is the secret to its moistness.

# Classic Apple Pie

**Yield: 8 slices**

## Crust
**3**    CUPS ALL-PURPOSE FLOUR
**2**    TEASPOONS GRATED LEMON ZEST
     (1 MEDIUM LEMON)
**2**    STICKS (1 CUP) SALTED BUTTER, CHILLED
**6**    TO 8 TABLESPOONS ICE WATER

## Filling
**6**    LARGE GRANNY SMITH APPLES, PEELED AND
     THINLY SLICED (ABOUT 4 CUPS)
**1**    CUP GRANULATED SUGAR
**1**    TEASPOON GROUND CINNAMON
**¼**    CUP CORNSTARCH
**½**    STICK (¼ CUP) SALTED BUTTER, CHILLED AND
     CUT INTO SMALL PIECES

## Egg Wash
**1**    LARGE EGG, BEATEN
**1**    TABLESPOON GRANULATED SUGAR

**1**   To prepare crust: Mix flour and lemon zest together with wire whisk in a medium bowl. With pastry cutter or 2 knives, cut in butter with flour until dough resembles coarse meal.

**2**   Add ice water and blend until dough can be gathered into a ball. Divide dough in half, flatten into disks, and wrap tightly in plastic wrap or a plastic bag. Refrigerate 1 hour or until firm.

**3**   To prepare filling: Combine sugar, cinnamon and cornstarch with a wire whisk in a large bowl. Add apples to sugar mixture and toss with a wooden spoon until dry ingredients coat the apples completely.

**4**   Preheat oven to 400°F.

**5**   On a floured surface use a floured rolling pin to roll out one piece of dough into a circle 11 inches in diameter. Fold the crust in half, then in quarters.

**6**   Place point of folded crust in center of a 9-inch pie plate and carefully unfold. Trim excess dough, leaving about ¾ inch hanging over edge of plate

**7**   Spoon in the apple filling and sprinkle the butter pieces on top.

**8**   To prepare top crust: Roll out second piece of dough into a circle 10 inches in diameter. Again, fold in half, then quarters, and place on top of filling. Fold extra crust of the top layer over the bottom layer. Crimp layers together decoratively.

**9**   Cut several steam slits in pie top, brush with egg wash, and sprinkle with 1 tablespoon sugar.

**10**   Place pie on center rack of oven. Bake for 20 minutes, then reduce heat to 350°F. Bake an additional 30 minutes, or until crust is deep golden brown and filling is bubbling through steam slits.

**11**   Remove from oven and cool to room temperature on rack.

---

**PREPARATION TIP**

After spooning in the apple filling, cover pie with the top crust. Trim excess dough with a paring knife, leaving about ¾ inch hanging over. Fold the extra crust of the top layer over the bottom layer and crimp layers together decoratively. Before baking, cut small vent slits in the top crust to allow steam to escape.

# Carrot Cake

**Yield: 12 to 16 servings**

## Cake

| | |
|---|---|
| **2½** | CUPS ALL-PURPOSE FLOUR |
| **2** | TEASPOONS BAKING SODA |
| **¼** | TEASPOON SALT |
| **2** | TEASPOONS CINNAMON |
| **1** | CUP LIGHT BROWN SUGAR, PACKED |
| **1** | CUP GRANULATED SUGAR |
| **3** | STICKS (1½ CUPS) SALTED BUTTER, SOFTENED |
| **3** | LARGE EGGS |
| **2** | TEASPOONS VANILLA EXTRACT |
| **3** | CUPS GRATED CARROT (3 TO 4 MEDIUM CARROTS) |
| **½** | CUP CRUSHED PINEAPPLE, DRAINED |
| **1** | CUP (6 OUNCES) RAISINS |
| **1** | CUP (4 OUNCES) CHOPPED WALNUTS |

## Icing

| | |
|---|---|
| **16** | OUNCES CREAM CHEESE, SOFTENED |
| **1** | STICK (½ CUP) SALTED BUTTER, SOFTENED |
| **1** | TABLESPOON FRESH LEMON JUICE (ABOUT 1 LARGE LEMON) |
| **2** | TEASPOONS VANILLA EXTRACT |
| **3** | CUPS POWDERED SUGAR |

**1** Preheat oven to 350°F. Grease and flour two 9-inch cake pans.

**2** In a large bowl stir together flour, baking soda, salt, cinnamon and sugars. Add butter, one egg and vanilla; blend with electric mixer on low speed. Increase speed to medium and beat for 2 minutes.

**3** Scrape down sides of bowl. Add remaining eggs, one at a time, beating 30 seconds after each addition. Add carrots, pineapple, raisins and walnuts. Blend on low until thoroughly combined.

**4** Pour batter into prepared pans and smooth the surface with a rubber spatula. Bake in center of oven for 60 to 70 minutes. Toothpick inserted into center should come out clean. Cool in pans for 10 minutes. Then invert cakes on rack and cool to room temperature.

**5** To prepare icing: On a medium bowl with electric mixer on medium speed, beat cream cheese and butter until smooth. Add lemon juice and vanilla; beat until combined. Add sugar gradually, mixing on low until smooth.

**6** To ice the carrot cake: Place one layer on a cake platter, and with a metal spatula spread icing over the top to form a thin filling. Place second layer over the first, rounded side up. Coat the top and sides of the cake evenly with remaining icing. Refrigerate for 1 hour to set icing.

# "Light" Chocolate Cheesecake

**Yield: 10 servings**

## Crust
**1** CUP CHOCOLATE WAFER COOKIE CRUMBS
**2** TABLESPOONS GRANULATED SUGAR
**1** TABLESPOON WATER

## Filling
**1** CUP (PACKED) DARK BROWN SUGAR
**¼** CUP UNSWEETENED COCOA POWDER
**¼** CUP ALL-PURPOSE FLOUR
**16** OUNCES NONFAT CREAM CHEESE
**1** CUP LIGHT SOUR CREAM
**4** LARGE EGG WHITES
**1½** OUNCES GERMAN SWEET CHOCOLATE, MELTED AND COOLED
**2** TEASPOONS VANILLA EXTRACT

**1** Preheat the oven to 300°F. Spray the sides and bottom of an 8½-inch springform pan with nonstick cooking spray. Place a shallow roasting pan of water on the bottom rack of the oven.

**2** Prepare the crust: In a medium bowl, use your fingers or a fork to toss the cookie crumbs with the granulated sugar and water until evenly moistened. Press the crumb mix-ture into the bottom and one-third of the way up the sides of the springform pan.

**3** Make the filling: In a small bowl, blend the brown sugar, cocoa, and flour. In a food processor, process the cream cheese and flour-cocoa mixture until smooth. Add the sour cream and blend until smooth. Add the egg whites and blend. Add the melted chocolate and vanilla and blend.

**4** Pour the filling into the crust and place the cheesecake on the center rack of the oven. Bake for 1 hour, or until the filling is just set (it will still be wobbly in the center). Turn off the heat but leave the cake in the oven for an-other 30 minutes. Remove from the oven and cool in the pan on a wire rack. Cover and re-frigerate until well chilled, at least 8 hours or overnight.

**5** To serve, run a knife around the edges of the cake to loosen it from the side of the springform, then remove the sides of the pan.

# Skinny Fallen Mousse Cake with Berry Sauce

**Yield: 12 servings**

## Cake

| | |
|---|---|
| ¼ | CUP WHOLE ALMONDS, TOASTED |
| ¾ | CUP GRANULATED SUGAR |
| ½ | CUP UNSWEETENED COCOA POWDER, SIFTED |
| 5 | TABLESPOONS BOILING WATER |
| 2 | OUNCES SWEET CHOCOLATE, FINELY CHOPPED |
| 1 | TEASPOON VANILLA EXTRACT |
| 2 | LARGE EGGS, SEPARATED, PLUS 2 EGG WHITES |
| 3 | TABLESPOONS ALL-PURPOSE FLOUR |
| ¼ | TEASPOON CREAM OF TARTAR |

## Berry Sauce

| | |
|---|---|
| 3 | CUPS WHOLE STRAWBERRIES |
| 2 | CUPS RASPBERRIES |
| | POWDERED SUGAR, FOR DUSTING |

**1** Make the cake: Preheat the oven to 375°F. Line the bottom of an 8½-inch springform pan with a circle of wax paper. Lightly spray the wax paper and sides of the pan with non-stick cooking spray.

**2** In a food processor, grind the toasted almonds for 2 to 3 seconds, or just until ground; do not overprocess or the nuts will be oily.

**3** In a double boiler, blend ½ cup of the sugar with the cocoa and 2 tablespoons of the boiling water. Add the 3 remaining tablespoons boiling water and stir until smooth. Add the sweet chocolate and stir over hot, not simmering, water, until the chocolate is melted. Stir in the vanilla, remove from the heat, and set aside.

**4** In a small bowl, beat the egg yolks until thick and pale. Whisk about ¼ cup of the chocolate mixture into the eggs to warm them. Transfer the warmed eggs to the chocolate mixture and stir to combine. Stir in the flour and ground almonds and set aside.

**5** In a large bowl, beat the 4 egg whites until foamy. Add the cream of tartar and beat until soft peaks form. Add the remaining ¼ cup sugar and beat until stiff peaks form.

**6** Stir one-fourth of the egg whites into the chocolate mixture to lighten it, then gently but thoroughly fold in the remaining egg whites. Spread the batter in the prepared pan and bake for 25 minutes, or until a cake tester inserted in the center comes out clean. Set the pan on a wire rack to cool completely.

**7** Make the sauce: In a food processor, purée 2 cups of the strawberries and 1 cup of the raspberries. Strain through a fine-mesh sieve to remove the seeds. Slice the remaining 1 cup strawberries and stir the sliced strawberries and remaining raspberries into the strained purée.

**8** To serve, remove the sides of the pan. Dust with powdered sugar, cut into 12 wedges, and serve the berry sauce on the side.

# Super Mud Pie

**Yield: 8 to 10 servings**

## Crust

| | |
|---|---|
| **2** | CUPS CHOCOLATE WAFER CRUMBS |
| **½** | STICK (¼ CUP) UNSALTED BUTTER, MELTED |

## Caramel Sauce

| | |
|---|---|
| **½** | CUP GRANULATED SUGAR |
| **3** | TABLESPOONS WATER |
| **½** | CUP HEAVY CREAM, SCALDED |
| **½** | STICK (¼ CUP) UNSALTED BUTTER, SOFTENED |

## Espresso Fudge Sauce

| | |
|---|---|
| **4** | OUNCES SEMISWEET CHOCOLATE, COARSELY CHOPPED |
| **¼** | CUP UNSWEETENED COCOA POWDER |
| **½** | STICK (¼ CUP) UNSALTED BUTTER |
| **¾** | CUP FRESHLY BREWED ESPRESSO |
| **¾** | CUP GRANULATED SUGAR |
| **¼** | CUP LIGHT CORN SYRUP |
| **1** | TABLESPOON COFFEE LIQUEUR |

## Assembly

| | |
|---|---|
| **1** | QUART VANILLA ICE CREAM, SOFTENED |
| **½** | CUP COARSELY CHOPPED TOASTED MACADAMIA NUTS |

**1** Make the crust: Combine the wafer crumbs and melted butter. Press the crumb-and-butter mixture into the bottom and partially up the sides of a 9-inch springform pan.

**2** Make the caramel sauce: In a small heavy saucepan, dissolve the sugar in the water over low heat, stirring constantly. Bring to a boil over medium-high heat, then let boil without stirring until the syrup turns a light amber. While the syrup is boiling, brush down the sides of the pan from time to time to prevent crystals from forming. Remove the pan from the heat and stir in the hot cream (be careful, it will bubble rapidly). Continue stirring, over low heat if necessary, until all of the caramel is dissolved into the cream. Stir in the butter and set aside to cool slightly. Pour the warm caramel sauce over the crust and freeze the crust until firm, about 30 minutes.

**3** Make the espresso fudge sauce: In a medium saucepan, combine the chopped chocolate, cocoa, butter, and espresso. Stir over low heat until smooth. Add the sugar and corn syrup, increase the heat to medium, and stir until the sugar dissolves. Increase the heat until the sauce reaches a low boil. Cook without stirring until the sauce thickens, 12 to 15 minutes. Remove from the heat and stir in the coffee liqueur.

**4** Cool the sauce to room temperature, then pour 1 cup of the sauce over the caramel layer and return the crust to the freezer. Set the remaining sauce aside and keep just warm enough so it remains pourable.

**5** Assemble the pie: Spread the softened ice cream over the caramel layer and return to the freezer to firm, about 1 hour. Pour the remaining fudge sauce over the ice cream layer, top with the macadamia nuts, and freeze until firm, about 2 hours.

**6** Serve: Wrap a hot, wet towel around the springform for 2 minutes to loosen, then remove the sides of the pan.

# Chocolate Chip Cheesecake

**Yield: 12 to 16 servings**

## Crust

**5** OUNCES CHOCOLATE COOKIE CRUMBS (ABOUT 1 CUP)

**2** TABLESPOONS SALTED BUTTER, SOFTENED

## Filling

**16** OUNCES CREAM CHEESE, SOFTENED

**1** CUP GRANULATED SUGAR

**16** OUNCES SOUR CREAM (ABOUT 2 CUPS)

**3** LARGE EGGS

**1** TABLESPOON VANILLA EXTRACT

**9** OUNCES SEMISWEET CHOCOLATE CHIPS, DIVIDED (ABOUT 1½ CUPS)

**1** Preheat oven to 350°F.

**2** Prepare the crust: Grind cookies into fine crumbs using a blender or a food processor fitted with a metal blade. Add butter and blend until smooth. Press crust into bottom of 9-inch springform pan, and refrigerate while preparing the filling.

**3** Prepare the filling: Beat cream cheese until smooth in a large bowl using an electric mixer. Blend in sugar and sour cream. Add the eggs and vanilla, and mix until smooth.

**4** Using a wooden spoon, stir in 1 cup of the chocolate chips. Pour filling into the crust-lined pan, and smooth top with a spatula. Sprinkle the remaining ½ cup chocolate chips evenly over the top. Bake 30 to 40 minutes. Turn oven off and leave cheesecake in oven for 1 hour to set. Remove from oven and chill in refrigerator until firm, about 3 to 4 hours.

# Chocolate Chip Banana Bread

**Yield: Two 9-inch loaves**

**3** CUPS ALL-PURPOSE FLOUR

**2** TEASPOONS BAKING POWDER

**1** TEASPOON SALT

**1½** STICKS (¾ CUP) UNSALTED BUTTER, SOFTENED

**2** CUPS GRANULATED SUGAR

**3** CUPS MASHED BANANAS (ABOUT 8)

**4** LARGE EGGS, WELL BEATEN

**2** TEASPOONS VANILLA EXTRACT

**1** CUP MINI SEMISWEET CHOCOLATE CHIPS

**1** Preheat the oven to 350°F. Lightly butter two 9-by-5-inch loaf pans. Line the bottoms with buttered parchment or wax paper.

**2** In a bowl, whisk together the flour, baking powder, and salt.

**3** In a medium bowl, cream the butter and sugar. Add the bananas and eggs, beating until well blended. Beat in the vanilla.

**4** Add the dry ingredients to the banana mixture and blend well. Stir in the semisweet chocolate chips. Do not overmix.

**5** Pour the batter into the prepared pans and bake for 55 to 60 minutes, or until golden brown and a cake tester inserted in the center comes out clean. Set the pans on a rack to cool for 15 minutes. Then turn out of the pans to cool completely.

# Ganache-Filled Devil's Food Cake

**Yield: One 9-inch layer cake**

## Cake
**1¾** CUPS BOILING WATER
**6** OUNCES SEMISWEET CHOCOLATE, COARSELY CHOPPED
**1** CUP UNSWEETENED COCOA POWDER
**2** CUPS SIFTED CAKE FLOUR
**2** TEASPOONS BAKING SODA
**¼** TEASPOON SALT
**10** OUNCES UNSALTED BUTTER, SOFTENED
**1¾** CUPS (PACKED) DARK BROWN SUGAR
**4** LARGE EGGS
**2** TEASPOONS VANILLA EXTRACT

## Chocolate Ganache
**½** CUP HEAVY CREAM
**2** TABLESPOONS UNSALTED BUTTER
**4** OUNCES SEMISWEET CHOCOLATE, FINELY CHOPPED

## Chocolate Frosting
**2½** STICKS (1¼ CUPS) PLUS 2 TABLESPOONS UNSALTED BUTTER, SOFTENED
**4½** CUPS POWDERED SUGAR
**1** CUP UNSWEETENED COCOA POWDER
**2** TEASPOONS VANILLA EXTRACT
**¼** CUP PLUS 2 TABLESPOONS MILK

**1** Make the cake: Preheat the oven to 350°F. Butter two 9-inch cake pans. Line the bottoms with circles of wax paper, then butter and flour the paper.

**2** In a medium bowl, pour the boiling water over the chopped chocolate. Set aside for 5 minutes. Add the cocoa and stir until the mixture is smooth. Set aside to cool to room temperature.

**3** In a small bowl, whisk together the flour, baking soda, and salt.

**4** In a large bowl with an electric mixer, cream the butter and brown sugar. Add the eggs one at a time, beating well after each addition. Beat in the vanilla. Add the flour mixture and half of the chocolate mixture. Beat on low speed to combine, then on high for 1½ minutes. Add the remaining chocolate mixture and beat the batter on low speed to combine.

**5** Pour the batter into the prepared pans and bake for 30 to 40 minutes, or until a cake tester inserted in the center comes out clean. Set the cake pans on a wire rack to cool for 20 minutes. Then invert the cakes onto the racks to cool completely.

**6** Prepare the ganache: In a small saucepan, bring the cream and butter to a simmer. Add the chocolate, cover for 5 minutes, then stir until smooth. Refrigerate the ganache until firm enough to spread.

**7** Meanwhile, make the frosting: In a large bowl with an electric mixer, cream the butter. In a medium bowl, whisk together the sugar and cocoa. Beat one-third of the sugar-cocoa mixture into the butter. Mix in the vanilla. Add the rest of the sugar-cocoa mixture alternately with the milk and beat until the frosting is smooth.

**8** Assemble the cake: Top one cake layer with the ganache. Add the second layer of cake and frost the sides of the cake, then the top. Decoratively pipe frosting around the base and top edges of the cake.

# Chocolate Coconut Pecan Pie

**Yield: One 9-inch pie**

## Crust

| | |
|---|---|
| **1** | CUP ALL-PURPOSE FLOUR |
| **⅛** | TEASPOON SALT |
| **6** | TABLESPOONS COLD UNSALTED BUTTER, CUT INTO PIECES |
| **2** | TO 3 TABLESPOONS ICE WATER |

## Filling and Topping

| | |
|---|---|
| **2** | TABLESPOONS ALL-PURPOSE FLOUR |
| **¼** | TEASPOON BAKING POWDER |
| **¼** | TEASPOON SALT |
| **½** | STICK (¼ CUP) UNSALTED BUTTER |
| **¾** | CUP (PACKED) LIGHT BROWN SUGAR |
| **4** | LARGE EGG YOLKS |
| **2** | TEASPOONS VANILLA EXTRACT |
| **1** | CUP SHREDDED COCONUT |
| **1** | CUP COARSELY CHOPPED PECANS |
| **4** | OUNCES SEMISWEET CHOCOLATE, COARSELY CHOPPED |
| **¾** | CUP HEAVY CREAM |
| | WHOLE PECANS AND WHIPPED CREAM, FOR GARNISH |

**1** Make the crust: In a small bowl, whisk together the flour and salt. With a pastry blender, incorporate the butter into the flour until the mixture resembles coarse meal. Toss the mixture with a fork, sprinkling on just enough of the ice water to form a cohesive dough. Flatten the dough into a disk, wrap in plastic wrap, and chill in the refrigerator for 30 minutes. Roll out to a 12-inch circle and fit into a 9-inch pie plate. Trim and crimp the edges. Return to the refrigerator while you make the filling.

**2** Preheat the oven to 350°F.

**3** Prepare the filling: In a small bowl, whisk together the flour, baking powder, and salt. In a medium bowl with an electric mixer, cream the butter and sugar. Beat in the egg yolks and the vanilla. Slowly beat in the flour mixture. Stir in the coconut, pecans, and half of the chopped chocolate. Blend in the cream until smooth.

**4** Pour the filling into the pie crust and sprinkle with the remaining chopped chocolate. Bake for 40 to 45 minutes, or until the crust is golden brown. The center of the filling will still be a bit jiggly. Let cool to room temperature, then chill for 2 hours to set.

**5** Garnish each slice of pie with a whole pecan and a whipped cream rosette.

# Chocolate Pumpkin Pie

**Yield: One 9-inch pie**

## Crust

| | |
|---|---|
| **6** | TABLESPOONS COLD UNSALTED BUTTER |
| **1** | CUP ALL-PURPOSE FLOUR |
| ¼ | TEASPOON SALT |
| **2** | TO 3 TABLESPOONS ICE WATER |

## Pumpkin Filling

| | |
|---|---|
| **1** | CUP (PACKED) LIGHT BROWN SUGAR |
| **1** | TABLESPOON PLUS 1 TEASPOON ALL-PURPOSE FLOUR |
| **1** | TEASPOON CINNAMON |
| ¼ | TEASPOON GRATED NUTMEG |
| ¼ | TEASPOON SALT |
| ½ | TEASPOON GROUND GINGER |
| ⅛ | TEASPOON GROUND CLOVES |
| **1** | LARGE EGG |
| **1** | LARGE EGG WHITE |
| **2** | TABLESPOONS VANILLA EXTRACT |
| **1** | 15-OUNCE CAN UNSWEETENED SOLID-PACK PUMPKIN PURÉE |
| **1** | CUP LIGHT CREAM OR HALF-AND-HALF |

## Chocolate Topping

| | |
|---|---|
| **4** | OUNCES SEMISWEET CHOCOLATE, COARSELY CHOPPED |
| ½ | CUP HEAVY CREAM |
| **2** | TABLESPOONS GRANULATED SUGAR |

**1** Make the crust: With a pastry blender, incorporate the butter into the flour until the mixture resembles coarse meal. Toss the mixture with a fork, sprinkling on just enough of the ice water to form a cohesive dough. Flatten the dough into a disk, wrap in plastic wrap, and chill in the refrigerator for 45 minutes. Roll out to an 11-inch circle and fit into a 9-inch pie plate. Trim and crimp the edges. Return to the refrigerator while you make the filling.

**2** Preheat the oven to 350°F.

**3** Prepare the pumpkin filling: In a medium bowl with an electric mixer, beat the brown sugar, flour, cinnamon, nutmeg, salt, ginger, and cloves until well mixed. Beat in the egg, egg white, and vanilla until smooth. Beat in the pumpkin, then the light cream. Pour into the chilled pastry shell. Bake for 40 minutes, or until the center is set. Cool on a rack to room temperature.

**4** Meanwhile, make the chocolate topping: Place the chocolate in a small bowl. In a small saucepan, bring the heavy cream and the granulated sugar to a simmer, then stir until the sugar is dissolved. Pour the hot cream over the chocolate. Let stand, covered, for 5 minutes, then stir until smooth. Chill the chocolate topping mixture until thickened but still pourable, about 30 minutes.

**5** Pour the chocolate over the pumpkin layer and chill the pie until the chocolate is set, about 1 hour.

# Mrs. Fields' Macadamia Nut Tart

**Yield: 12 servings**

## Pastry Crust

| | |
|---|---|
| **1¾** | CUPS ALL-PURPOSE FLOUR |
| **¼** | CUP GRANULATED SUGAR |
| **1** | STICK (½ CUP) SALTED BUTTER, CHILLED |
| **2** | LARGE EGG YOLKS |
| **3** | TABLESPOONS ICE WATER |

## Filling

| | |
|---|---|
| **1** | CUP CORN SYRUP |
| **1** | STICK (½ CUP) PLUS 3 TABLESPOONS SALTED BUTTER |
| **1** | CUP GRANULATED SUGAR |
| **2** | TABLESPOONS UNSULFURIZED MOLASSES |
| **¼** | TEASPOON SALT |
| **2** | LARGE EGGS, LIGHTLY BEATEN |
| **1** | TEASPOON VANILLA EXTRACT |
| **2½** | CUPS UNSALTED DRY-ROASTED MACADAMIA NUTS |
| | WHIPPED CREAM (OPTIONAL) |

**1** Prepare the crust: Combine flour, sugar, and butter, and work with a pastry cutter until dough resembles coarse meal. Add egg yolks and water, and mix with a fork just until dough can be shaped into a ball. Or, using a food processor fitted with a metal blade, combine flour, sugar, and butter. Process until dough resembles coarse meal. Add egg yolks and water and process just until a ball begins to form.

**PREPARATION TIP**

Fold the dough in half, then drape it over the prepared tart pan (*right, top*). Gently press the dough into the pan. Be sure that there is enough dough pressed into the fluted edges to support the filling when baked. Use a rolling pin to roll off the excess dough (*right, bottom*).

**2** Shape dough into a disk and wrap tightly in plastic wrap or plastic bag. Chill in refrigerator 1 hour or until firm.

**3** Prepare the filling: Combine the corn syrup, butter, sugar, molasses, and salt in a double boiler. Bring to a boil over medium heat, stirring occasionally. Remove from heat and cool to room temperature. Once cool, add the eggs and vanilla and stir until smooth. Set syrup mixture aside until ready to use. (Mixture can be made up to 2 days in advance and refrigerated until it is ready to use.)

**4** Assemble the tart: Preheat oven to 300°F. Spray nonstick cooking spray on an 8- or 9-inch tart pan with a removable bottom.

**5** On a floured board using a floured rolling pin, roll out dough to a 10-inch circle, ¼ inch thick. Place pastry in pan, lightly pressing it into the bottom and sides. Roll off excess dough from the top edge with rolling pin.

**6** Fill the pastry shell with the macadamia nuts. Pour filling over nuts and bake 90 minutes or until golden brown. Let pie cool, remove sides of pan and garnish with whipped cream, if desired.

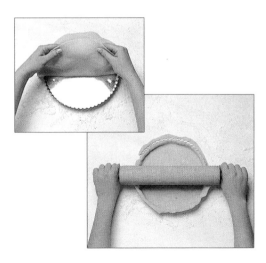

# Milk Chocolate Toffee Cream Pie

**Yield: One 9-inch pie**

## Crust

**1½** CUPS CHOCOLATE WAFER CRUMBS
**5** TABLESPOONS (¼ CUP PLUS 1 TABLESPOON) UNSALTED BUTTER, MELTED
**2** TABLESPOONS GRANULATED SUGAR

## Filling

**6** OUNCES MILK CHOCOLATE, COARSELY CHOPPED
**¾** CUP HEAVY CREAM
**8** OUNCES CREAM CHEESE, SOFTENED
**¼** CUP (PACKED) LIGHT BROWN SUGAR
**1** TABLESPOON VANILLA EXTRACT
**¾** CUP CHOPPED CHOCOLATE-COVERED TOFFEE CANDY

**1** Preheat the oven to 350°F.

**2** Make the crust: In a medium bowl, combine the wafer crumbs, butter, and sugar. Press the mixture into the bottom and up the sides of a 9-inch pie plate. Bake for 10 minutes. Place on a wire rack to cool.

**3** Prepare the filling: Place the chocolate in a small bowl. In a small saucepan, bring ½ cup of the cream to a simmer. Pour the hot cream over the chocolate. Let stand, covered, for 5 minutes, then stir until smooth.

**4** In a medium bowl with an electric mixer, beat the cream cheese, sugar, and vanilla until smooth. Beat in the remaining ¼ cup cream. Gently beat in the cooled chocolate mixture. Fold in ½ cup of the chopped toffee candy.

**5** Pour the filling into the cooled crust, and sprinkle with the remaining ¼ cup of chopped toffee. Chill until firm, about 2 hours.

# Debbi's Deadly Chocolate Muffins

**Yield: 12 muffins**

**12** OUNCES SEMISWEET CHOCOLATE, COARSELY CHOPPED
**1** STICK (½ CUP) UNSALTED BUTTER
**½** CUP SOUR CREAM
**1** CUP SIFTED CAKE FLOUR
**½** TEASPOON BAKING SODA
**¼** TEASPOON SALT
**4** LARGE EGGS
**½** CUP (PACKED) LIGHT BROWN SUGAR
**1** TEASPOON VANILLA EXTRACT
**1¼** CUPS SEMISWEET CHOCOLATE CHIPS
**¼** CUP COARSELY CHOPPED MACADAMIA NUTS
**¼** CUP WHITE CHOCOLATE CHIPS

**1** Preheat the oven to 350°F. Lightly oil the top surface of a 12-cup muffin tin. Line the cups with paper liners.

**2** In a double boiler, melt the chopped semisweet chocolate with the butter and stir until smooth. Remove from the heat and stir in the sour cream.

**3** In a small bowl, whisk together the flour, baking soda, and salt.

**4** In a large bowl with an electric mixer, beat the eggs and sugar until light and pale, about 5 minutes. Beat in the chocolate mixture and the vanilla. Add the flour mixture and 1 cup of the semisweet chocolate chips.

**5** Spoon the batter evenly into the prepared muffin cups. Top with the remaining ¼ cup semisweet chips, the macadamia nuts, and the white chocolate chips. Bake for 20 to 25 minutes, or until the centers are set.

**6** Set the muffin tin on a wire rack to cool for 15 minutes. Then remove the muffins to cool completely.

# The Ultimate Ice Cream Pie

**Yield: One 9-inch pie**

## Cookie Crumb Crust

**1¼** CUPS CHOCOLATE-CHIP COOKIE CRUMBS

## Fudge Sauce

**2** OUNCES SEMISWEET CHOCOLATE, CHOPPED
**2½** TABLESPOONS UNSALTED BUTTER
**¼** CUP PLUS 2 TABLESPOONS
    GRANULATED SUGAR
**2** TABLESPOONS UNSWEETENED COCOA POWDER
**2** TABLESPOONS CORN SYRUP
**¼** CUP PLUS 2 TABLESPOONS WATER
**1** TEASPOON VANILLA EXTRACT

## Caramel Sauce

**½** CUP GRANULATED SUGAR
**2** TABLESPOONS WATER
**¼** CUP CREAM, SCALDED
**2** TABLESPOONS UNSALTED BUTTER, SOFTENED

## Filling

**1** CUP MINI MARSHMALLOWS
**1** CUP SEMISWEET CHOCOLATE CHIPS
**3** CUPS VANILLA ICE CREAM,
    SOFTENED IN THE REFRIGERATOR

**1** Preheat the oven to 325°F.

**2** Make the crust: Press the cookie crumbs into the bottom and up the sides of a 9-inch pie plate. Bake for 10 minutes. Cool the crust to room temperature.

**3** Prepare the fudge sauce: In a small saucepan, melt the chocolate and butter over low heat; stir until smooth. Add the sugar, cocoa, corn syrup, and water and cook until the sugar dissolves. Bring the mixture to a boil and cook at a low boil, without stirring, until the sauce is thick and smooth, about 15 minutes. Remove from the heat and stir in the vanilla. Set aside to cool to lukewarm.

**4** Make the caramel sauce: In a heavy medium saucepan, dissolve the sugar in the water over low heat, stirring constantly. Bring to a boil over medium-high heat, then let boil, without stirring, until the syrup turns a light amber. While the syrup is boiling, brush down the sides of the pan from time to time with a wet pastry brush to prevent crystals from forming. Remove the pan from the heat and stir in the hot cream (it will bubble rapidly). Stir in the butter and continue stirring the sauce until smooth. Cool the sauce to lukewarm.

**5** Assemble: Pour the fudge sauce into the pie crust. Chill in the freezer until the sauce is set, about 15 minutes. In a medium bowl, stir the marshmallows and chocolate chips into the softened ice cream. Spread the ice cream mixture over the fudge layer and smooth the top. Place in the freezer until set, about 30 minutes.

**6** Dip a fork into the caramel sauce and drizzle it in a crisscross pattern over the top of the pie. Return to the freezer for 1 hour to set. Cut the pie into wedges with a sharp knife and serve immediately.

# Fallen Soufflé

## Yield: 8 servings

| | |
|---|---|
| **6** | TABLESPOONS UNSALTED BUTTER, SOFTENED |
| ¾ | CUP GRANULATED SUGAR |
| ½ | CUP ALL-PURPOSE FLOUR |
| **4** | OUNCES SEMISWEET CHOCOLATE, FINELY CHOPPED |
| ½ | CUP HEAVY CREAM |
| **4** | LARGE EGGS, SEPARATED |
| | PINCH OF SALT |
| | POWDERED SUGAR, FOR DUSTING |
| | VANILLA ICE CREAM, FOR SERVING |

**1** Preheat the oven to 350°F. Butter and sugar a 2-quart, 8-inch-diameter soufflé dish.

**2** In a medium bowl with an electric mixer, cream the butter and ½ cup of the sugar until light and fluffy. Beat in the flour until blended.

**3** In a double boiler, melt the chocolate with the cream, stirring frequently until smooth. Slowly beat the chocolate cream into the butter-sugar mixture, then return the chocolate mixture to the double boiler. Cook over medium-low heat, stirring constantly, for 7 to 8 minutes, or until thickened. Remove from the heat.

**4** In a large bowl, lightly beat the egg yolks. Whisk one-fourth of the hot chocolate mixture into the egg yolks to warm them. Return the warmed egg yolk mixture to the saucepan.

**5** In a medium bowl, beat the egg whites with the salt until foamy. Slowly add the remaining ¼ cup sugar and beat until stiff, glossy peaks form. Stir one-fourth of the egg whites into the chocolate batter to lighten it. Gently and thoroughly fold in the remaining egg whites.

**6** Spoon the batter into the prepared dish. Set the dish in a deep baking pan and fill the pan with 1 inch of lukewarm water. Bake in the water bath for 1 hour and 10 minutes, or until puffed.

**7** Remove from the water bath and let stand for 15 minutes, then loosen the edges and invert the soufflé onto a serving plate. Chill until serving time.

**8** Cut the fallen soufflé into wedges, dust with powdered sugar, and serve with a scoop of vanilla ice cream.

# Chocolate Banana Cream Pie

**Yield: 8 to 10 servings**

## Crust

**1**   CUP ALL-PURPOSE FLOUR
**2**   TABLESPOONS GRANULATED SUGAR
**½**   TEASPOON SALT
**6**   TABLESPOONS COLD UNSALTED BUTTER, CUT INTO PIECES
**1**   EGG YOLK
**2**   TABLESPOONS ICE WATER

## Filling

**¾**   CUP GRANULATED SUGAR
**5**   TABLESPOONS CORNSTARCH
**¼**   TEASPOON SALT
**1½**   CUPS HEAVY CREAM
**1**   CUP MILK
**5**   LARGE EGG YOLKS
**2**   LARGE EGGS
**6**   OUNCES SEMISWEET CHOCOLATE, COARSELY CHOPPED
**2**   TEASPOONS VANILLA EXTRACT
**3**   MEDIUM BANANAS
**1**   TABLESPOON FRESH LEMON JUICE
    WHIPPED CREAM, FOR GARNISH

**1** Prepare the crust: In a food processor, combine the flour, sugar, and salt and process briefly to combine. Add the butter and process until the mixture resembles coarse meal. With the machine running, add the egg yolk and ice water and process just until the dough masses together. Gather the dough into a ball, flatten into a large disk, and then press into a 9-inch pie plate; trim and crimp the edges. Freeze for 10 minutes.

**2** Preheat the oven to 425°F. Line the pie crust loosely with foil and fill with dried beans, rice or metal pie weights. Bake for 10 minutes. Reduce the oven temperature to 350°F, remove the weights and bake for 10 minutes longer, or until golden brown. Set the crust on a wire rack to cool completely.

**3** Make the filling: In a saucepan, combine the sugar, cornstarch, salt, cream, and milk. Bring to a simmer over medium heat, stirring constantly to dissolve the sugar, about 12 minutes. Remove from the heat.

**4** In a small bowl, beat the egg yolks and eggs. Whisk about ¼ cup of the cream mixture into the eggs to warm them. Transfer the warmed eggs to the saucepan. Cook over medium heat, stirring constantly, until the custard is of pudding consistency, about 6 minutes; do not boil. Remove from the heat, add the chocolate, and let stand for 1 minute. Add vanilla and stir until the chocolate is melted.

**5** Spread half of the custard in the cooled pie crust. Slice and arrange 1½ bananas over the custard. Top with the remaining custard. Slice the remaining 1½ bananas and toss the slices with the lemon juice; drain well. Arrange the banana slices over the custard. Cover the pie with plastic wrap and refrigerate until well chilled, about 4 hours.

**6** Serve the pie garnished with rosettes of whipped cream.

# Caramel Chocolate Tartlets

**Yield: 8 tartlets**

### PASTRY

**1½** CUPS ALL-PURPOSE FLOUR
**¼** CUP GRANULATED SUGAR
**1** STICK (½ CUP) SALTED BUTTER, CHILLED
**2** LARGE EGG YOLKS
**1** TEASPOON VANILLA EXTRACT
**4** TO 5 TABLESPOONS ICE WATER

### CARAMEL FILLING

**1½** STICKS (¾ CUP) SALTED BUTTER
**1** CUP (PACKED) DARK BROWN SUGAR
**⅓** CUP LIGHT CORN SYRUP
**3** TABLESPOONS HEAVY CREAM
**1** 16-OUNCE SOLID SEMISWEET OR MILK
CHOCOLATE BAR, AT ROOM TEMPERATURE

**1** Prepare pastry: In a medium bowl, combine flour, sugar, and butter with a pastry cutter until dough resembles coarse meal. Add egg yolks and vanilla. Gradually add ice water until dough can be shaped into a ball. Or, use a food processor fitted with a metal blade to combine flour, sugar, and butter until dough resembles coarse meal. Add egg yolks, vanilla, and ice water by tablespoons, and process until dough begins to form a ball.

**2** Flatten dough into a disk and wrap tightly in plastic wrap or place in plastic bag. Chill 1 hour or until firm.

**3** On floured board using a floured rolling pin, roll out dough to ¼ inch thickness. Cut 4-inch rounds to fit into 3½-inch-diameter tart pans. Gently press into tart pans and place in refrigerator for 15 minutes. Preheat oven to 400°F.

**4** Remove tart shells from refrigerator and prick bottom with a fork. Bake 13 to 15 minutes or until edges begin to turn golden brown. Cool tart shells to room temperature.

**5** Prepare the caramel filling: Combine butter, brown sugar, and corn syrup in a heavy 2-quart saucepan. Place over medium heat, and stir constantly until sugar dissolves. Turn heat to high and boil without stirring for 2 minutes, or until large bubbles form.

**6** Remove from heat and stir in cream. Cool caramel 5 minutes and then pour into tart shells. Cool caramel tartlets to room temperature. Use a vegetable peeler to slowly and carefully shave curls from the chocolate bar. Sprinkle tartlets with chocolate curls.

# Double-Fudge Chip Cake

**Yield: One 9-inch layer cake**

## Cake

**3**   OUNCES UNSWEETENED CHOCOLATE, FINELY CHOPPED

**2¼**  CUPS SIFTED CAKE FLOUR

**2**   TEASPOONS BAKING SODA

**½**   TEASPOON SALT

**1**   STICK (½ CUP) SALTED BUTTER, SOFTENED

**2¼**  CUPS (PACKED) LIGHT BROWN SUGAR

**3**   LARGE EGGS, AT ROOM TEMPERATURE

**1½** TEASPOONS VANILLA EXTRACT

**1**   CUP SOUR CREAM

**1**   CUP BOILING WATER

## Frosting

**8**   OUNCES UNSWEETENED CHOCOLATE, FINELY CHOPPED

**2**   STICKS (1 CUP) UNSALTED BUTTER, SOFTENED

**2**   POUNDS POWDERED SUGAR

**1**   CUP HEAVY CREAM

**4**   TEASPOONS VANILLA EXTRACT

**6**   OUNCES MILK CHOCOLATE CHIPS (1 CUP)

**1**   PACKAGE CHOCOLATE KISSES, FOR GARNISH

**1** Preheat the oven to 350°F. Grease and flour three 9-inch cake pans.

**2** Make the cake: In a double boiler, melt the chocolate over hot, not simmering, water. Set aside to cool.

**3** In a medium bowl, combine the flour, baking soda, and salt.

**4** In a large bowl with an electric mixer, cream the butter. Add the brown sugar and then the eggs, one at a time, blending well after each addition. Beat at high speed for 5 minutes. Beat in the vanilla and the melted chocolate.

**5** Beat in portions of the flour mixture alternately with the sour cream, beginning and ending with the flour mixture; beat well after each addition.

**6** Stir in the boiling water and pour the batter at once into the prepared pans. Bake for 35 minutes, or until the center springs back when touched lightly. Set the cake pans on a rack to cool for 10 minutes. Then invert the cakes onto the racks to cool completely.

**7** Prepare the frosting: In a double boiler, melt the chocolate with the butter. Set aside to cool to room temperature.

**8** In a medium bowl with an electric mixer, blend the powdered sugar, cream, and vanilla until smooth. Add the cooled chocolate mixture and mix at low speed until blended. Place the frosting in the refrigerator until thick and firm yet still easy to spread, 20 to 30 minutes.

**9** Assemble: Place one cake layer upside down on a cake dish. Spread one-fourth of frosting on top and sprinkle with ½ cup of the chips. Add a second cake layer upside down and frost with another one-fourth of the frosting and the remaining ½ cup chips. Add the top layer upside down and frost the top and sides of the cake with the remaining frosting. Garnish the cake with the chocolate kisses.

# Mocha Mousse Cheesecake

**Yield: 12 to 16 servings**

### Crust

**4**  OUNCES CHOCOLATE CHIP COOKIE CRUMBS
(ABOUT 1 CUP)

**2**  TABLESPOONS SALTED BUTTER, MELTED

### Filling

**24**  OUNCES CREAM CHEESE, SOFTENED

**½**  CUP GRANULATED SUGAR

**½**  CUP (PACKED) LIGHT BROWN SUGAR

**8**  OUNCES SOUR CREAM (ABOUT 1 CUP)

**3**  LARGE EGGS

**7**  OUNCES SEMISWEET CHOCOLATE CHIPS,
MELTED (ABOUT 1¼ CUPS)

**½**  CUP COFFEE, FRESHLY BREWED

**1**  TABLESPOON VANILLA EXTRACT

### Glaze

**5**  OUNCES SEMISWEET CHOCOLATE
(ABOUT ¾ CUP)

**½**  STICK (¼ CUP) SALTED BUTTER, SOFTENED

**1** Preheat oven to 350°F.

**2** Make the crust: Use a blender or a food processor with a metal blade to grind cookies into fine crumbs. Add butter and blend until smooth. Press crust into bottom of a 9-inch springform pan. Refrigerate while preparing mousse.

**3** Make the filling: In a large bowl with an electric mixer, beat the cream cheese until very smooth. Add sugars and sour cream, and blend thoroughly. Add eggs and beat until mixture is smooth.

**4** Add melted chocolate, coffee, and vanilla, again blending ingredients until smooth. Pour filling into prepared pan, and bake in middle of oven for 50 to 60 minutes.

**5** Turn off oven, crack door 1 inch, and leave cheesecake in oven 1 hour to set. Then remove from oven and cool to room temperature.

**6** Make the glaze: In a small saucepan melt chocolate and butter over low heat; stir until smooth. Pour glaze over top of cheesecake and smooth with a metal spatula. Refrigerate 3 to 4 hours or until firm. Cut and serve.

## PREPARATION TIP
When baked cheesecake has cooled, pour chocolate-butter glaze over the top, and smooth with a metal spatula to form a thin chocolate frosting.

# Poppy Seed Bundt Cake

**Yield: 24 servings**

**3**    CUPS CAKE FLOUR, SIFTED
**2**    CUPS GRANULATED SUGAR
**½**    TEASPOON SALT
**1**    TEASPOON BAKING POWDER
**3**    STICKS (1½ CUPS) SALTED BUTTER, SOFTENED
**½**    CUP (4 OUNCES) SOUR CREAM
**6**    LARGE EGGS
**⅓**    CUP CREAM SHERRY
**⅓**    CUP POPPY SEEDS

## Topping
**¼**    CUP POWDERED SUGAR

**1** Preheat oven to 350°F. Grease and flour a 3-quart fluted tube pan or bundt pan.

**2** In large bowl with an electric mixer blend flour, sugar, salt and baking powder on low until all ingredients are distributed equally. Add butter, sour cream and 3 of the eggs, and mix on medium until the dry ingredients are moistened. Beat on high for 2 minutes, then scrape bowl.

**3** Add remaining 3 eggs, one at a time, alternating with the sherry. Beat well after each addition. Blend in poppy seeds on low speed.

**4** Pour batter into prepared pan and bake for 50 to 60 minutes or until toothpick inserted into the center of cake comes out clean. Cool in pan 10 minutes, then invert cake onto a rack to cool. When cake has cooled completely, lightly dust top with powdered sugar.

# Peanut Butter Cream Pie

**Yield: One 9-inch pie**

## Chocolate Crust
**6**    OUNCES SEMISWEET CHOCOLATE CHIPS (ABOUT 1 CUP)
**5**    TABLESPOONS UNSALTED BUTTER
**2½**    CUPS CRISP RICE CEREAL
**¼**    CUP MINI SEMISWEET CHOCOLATE CHIPS

## Filling
**8**    OUNCES CREAM CHEESE, SOFTENED
**1**    14-OUNCE CAN SWEETENED CONDENSED MILK
**¾**    CUP CREAMY PEANUT BUTTER
**2**    TEASPOONS VANILLA EXTRACT
**1**    CUP HEAVY CREAM

## Topping
**3**    OUNCES MILK CHOCOLATE, FINELY CHOPPED
**2**    TABLESPOONS HEAVY CREAM
     MILK CHOCOLATE CURLS, FOR GARNISH

**1** Make the crust: In a double boiler, melt the 6 ounces of chocolate chips and butter over low heat. Remove from the heat and stir until smooth. Gently stir in the rice cereal until completely coated. Set aside to cool to lukewarm, then stir in the mini chips. Press into the bottom and up the sides of a buttered 9-inch pie plate. Chill for 30 minutes to set the chocolate.

**2** Prepare the filling: In a large bowl with an electric mixer, beat the cream cheese until fluffy. Beat in the condensed milk, peanut butter, and vanilla.

**3** In a medium bowl, beat the heavy cream until soft peaks form. Fold the whipped cream into the peanut butter mixture. Pour the filling into the crust.

**4** Make the topping: In a double boiler, melt the milk chocolate over hot, not simmering, water. Add the heavy cream and stir constantly until blended. Set aside to cool slightly, then drizzle the chocolate over the top of the pie. Refrigerate until firm, about 2 hours. Garnish with milk chocolate curls.

# Lemon Custard Cake

**Yield: One 9-inch layer cake**

### Cake

| | |
|---|---|
| **1½** | CUPS CAKE FLOUR |
| **1** | CUP GRANULATED SUGAR |
| **¾** | TEASPOON BAKING POWDER |
| **½** | TEASPOON SALT |
| **1½** | STICKS ( CUP) UNSALTED BUTTER, SOFTENED |
| **¼** | CUP SOUR CREAM |
| **2** | LARGE EGGS, AT ROOM TEMPERATURE |
| **¼** | CUP LEMON JUICE |
| **2** | TEASPOONS GRATED LEMON ZEST |
| **½** | TEASPOON LEMON EXTRACT |

### Vanilla Custard

| | |
|---|---|
| **1** | CUP HEAVY CREAM |
| **1** | LARGE EGG |
| **2** | LARGE EGG YOLKS |
| **⅓** | CUP GRANULATED SUGAR |
| **1** | TABLESPOON PLUS 2 TEASPOONS CORNSTARCH |
| **1** | TEASPOON VANILLA EXTRACT |

### Chocolate Ganache

| | |
|---|---|
| **6** | OUNCES SEMISWEET CHOCOLATE, FINELY CHOPPED |
| **¾** | CUP HEAVY CREAM |
| **2** | TABLESPOONS UNSALTED BUTTER |
| **2** | TABLESPOONS GRANULATED SUGAR |

**1** Preheat the oven to 350°F. Grease a 9-inch cake pan, line the bottom with a circle of wax paper, then grease and flour the paper.

**2** Make the cake: In a large bowl, mix the flour, sugar, baking powder, and salt. Add the butter, sour cream, and 1 egg. Mix until just blended. Add the remaining egg, the lemon juice, zest, and extract. Beat until smooth.

**3** Scrape batter into pan and bake for 40 to 45 minutes, or until top is golden and a cake tester inserted in the center comes out clean. Set the cake pan on a wire rack to cool for 20 minutes. Then invert cake onto rack to cool completely. Wrap cake in plastic wrap and chill in freezer until slightly firm, about 15 minutes.

**4** Meanwhile, make the custard: In a small saucepan, bring cream to a simmer. In a bowl, beat whole egg, egg yolks, sugar, and corn-starch together until light and lemon-colored, about 3 minutes. Gradually whisk hot cream into egg mixture to warm it. Transfer warmed egg mixture to saucepan and cook over medium heat, stirring constantly, until thick, about 2 minutes. Remove from heat and stir in vanilla. Strain the custard through a fine sieve and set in a large bowl of ice water to quick-cool to room temperature. Cover and refrigerate until thoroughly chilled.

**5** Prepare the ganache: Place the chocolate in a medium bowl. In a small saucepan, bring the cream and butter to a simmer. Stir in the sugar. Pour the hot cream mixture over the choco-late. Let stand, covered, for 5 minutes, then stir until smooth. Let cool to room temperature.

**6** Assemble: With a long serrated knife, slice chilled cake horizontally into two layers. Place bottom cake layer on a 9-inch cardboard round. Place layer on a rack set over a cookie sheet. Spread top of cake with the chilled vanilla custard. Gently top with the second cake layer. Spread the ganache evenly over sides and top of cake. Refrigerate for 20 minutes to set.

# Chocolate Raspberry Rhapsody

**Yield: 16 servings**

### Chocolate Ring

**1¼** CUPS SEMISWEET CHOCOLATE CHIPS
**1** CUP GRANULATED SUGAR
**½** CUP BOILING WATER
**2** STICKS (1 CUP) UNSALTED BUTTER, SOFTENED
**4** LARGE EGGS
**2** TABLESPOONS RASPBERRY LIQUEUR
**2** TEASPOONS VANILLA EXTRACT
**⅛** TEASPOON SALT

### Raspberry Cream

**1** CUP HEAVY CREAM
**2** TABLESPOONS SEEDLESS RED RASPBERRY JAM
**2** TABLESPOONS GRANULATED SUGAR
**2** TEASPOONS VANILLA EXTRACT
FRESH RASPBERRIES, FOR GARNISH

**1** Preheat the oven to 350°F. Spray a 5-cup ring mold with nonstick cooking spray.

**2** Make the chocolate ring: In a food processor, combine the chocolate chips and sugar, then process until finely chopped. Add the boiling water and process until melted and smooth. Add the butter in three additions, processing briefly each time. Add the eggs, liqueur, vanilla, and salt. Process until well blended.

**3** Pour the mixture into the prepared ring mold. Place the mold in a larger pan and fill the pan with 2 inches of boiling water. Bake for 1 hour, or until firm to the touch; a knife inserted into the center should come out clean.

**4** Remove the mold from the water bath and let cool for 1 hour on a rack. Cover and refrigerate for at least 3 hours.

**5** Make the raspberry cream: In a small bowl, beat the cream with the jam, sugar, and vanilla until soft peaks form.

**6** Assemble: Run a knife around the edges of the mold and invert the ring onto a serving dish. Pipe a ring of raspberry cream rosettes around the base of the ring. Fill the center of the ring with the remaining raspberry cream. Garnish the ring with fresh raspberries.

# Mocha Soufflé

## Yield: 8 servings

½   CUP MILK
1¼   CUPS GRANULATED SUGAR
6   OUNCES UNSWEETENED CHOCOLATE,
       FINELY CHOPPED
2   TEASPOONS INSTANT ESPRESSO GRANULES
6   LARGE EGG WHITES
4   LARGE EGG YOLKS
     POWDERED SUGAR, FOR DUSTING

**1** Preheat the oven to 350°F. Butter six 6-ounce soufflé dishes.

**2** In a medium saucepan, combine the milk and 1 cup of the sugar. Cook, stirring occasionally, over medium-low heat until the sugar dissolves, 5 to 10 minutes. Reduce the heat to low. Add the chocolate and coffee granules, then stir until the mixture is melted and smooth. Set aside to cool to lukewarm.

**3** In a large bowl, beat the egg whites until foamy. Slowly add the remaining ¼ cup sugar and beat until stiff but not dry peaks form. In a medium bowl, lightly beat the egg yolks.

**4** Whisk the chocolate mixture into the yolks until well blended. Whisk one-fourth of the egg whites into the chocolate mixture to lighten it. Gently and thoroughly fold in the remaining egg whites.

**5** Divide the mixture evenly among the prepared soufflé dishes. Bake for 10 to 12 minutes, or until puffed. Remove from the oven, dust with confectioners' sugar, and serve immediately.

# Chocolate Waffle Pillows

## Yield: About 3½ dozen

### Waffles

2   CUPS ALL-PURPOSE FLOUR
1   TEASPOON BAKING POWDER
1   CUP UNSWEETENED COCOA POWDER
2   STICKS (1 CUP) SALTED BUTTER, SOFTENED
2   CUPS GRANULATED SUGAR
5   LARGE EGGS
2   TEASPOONS VANILLA EXTRACT

### Toppings

⅓   CUP POWDERED SUGAR
⅓   CUP UNSWEETENED COCOA POWDER
1   CUP FRESH RASPBERRIES
1   PINT WHIPPING CREAM, WHIPPED
½   CUP CHOCOLATE SYRUP

**1** Grease and preheat waffle iron.

**2** In medium bowl combine flour, baking powder and cocoa. Mix well with a wire whisk. Set aside.

**3** In large bowl with an electric mixer cream butter and sugar. Add eggs and vanilla and beat at medium speed. Batter will appear slightly curdled. Scrape down the sides of the bowl, then add the flour mixture and blend on low speed until just combined. Do not overmix.

**4** Drop by rounded tablespoons onto hot waffle iron, using about one tablespoon per 4-by-4-inch square. Cook approximately 1 minute. Carefully transfer to cool surface.

**5** Use any of the following toppings singly or in combination: a dusting of powdered sugar and cocoa powder; fresh raspberries and whipped cream; a drizzle of chocolate syrup.

# White Ivory Cream Cake

**Yield: One 9-inch layer cake**

## Cake

| | |
|---|---|
| **8** | OUNCES WHITE CHOCOLATE, FINELY CHOPPED |
| **3** | CUPS SIFTED CAKE FLOUR |
| **2** | TEASPOONS BAKING POWDER |
| **½** | TEASPOON SALT |
| **1** | STICK (½ CUP) UNSALTED BUTTER |
| **1¼** | CUPS GRANULATED SUGAR |
| **3** | LARGE EGGS |
| **2** | TEASPOONS VANILLA EXTRACT |
| **1** | CUP PLUS 1 TABLESPOON MILK |

## Filling and Frosting

| | |
|---|---|
| **1½** | POUNDS WHITE CHOCOLATE, FINELY CHOPPED |
| **2½** | CUPS HEAVY CREAM |
| **6** | TABLESPOONS UNSALTED BUTTER |
| **½** | CUP COARSELY CHOPPED MACADAMIA NUTS |
| | WHOLE MACADAMIA NUTS AND STRAWBERRIES, FOR GARNISH |

**1** Preheat the oven to 350°F. Butter and flour two 9-inch cake pans.

**2** Make the cake: In a double boiler, melt the white chocolate over hot, not simmering, water. Set aside to cool slightly.

**3** In a medium bowl, whisk together the flour, baking powder, and salt.

**4** In a large bowl with an electric mixer, cream the butter and sugar. Beat in the eggs one at a time, beating well after each addition. On low speed, beat in the melted chocolate and the vanilla. In three additions, on low speed, alternately beat in the flour mixture and the milk. Beat until just smooth, about 20 seconds.

**5** Pour the batter into the prepared pans and bake for 25 to 30 minutes, or until the top is golden and a cake tester inserted in the center comes out clean. Set the cake pans on a wire rack to cool for 20 minutes. Then invert the cakes onto the racks to cool the layers completely.

**6** Prepare the filling and frosting: Place the white chocolate in a medium bowl. In a small heavy saucepan, bring 1½ cups of the cream and the butter to a simmer. Pour over the chocolate. Let stand, covered, for 5 minutes, then stir until smooth. Refrigerate the white chocolate mixture until firm enough to spread, about 1 hour.

**7** To assemble: Spread the bottom layer with 1 cup of the chilled white chocolate mixture. Arrange the chopped macadamia nuts over the filling. Top with the second cake layer.

**8** In a medium bowl, beat the remaining 1 cup cream until firm peaks form. Fold the whipped cream into the remaining white chocolate mixture. Spread this over the top and sides of the cake. Arrange whole macadamia nuts around the rim and base of the cake. Chill until ready to serve. Garnish each slice with a fanned whole strawberry.

# Chocolate Pecan Tartlets

**Yield: Twenty-four 2½-inch tartlets**

**Pastry**

| | |
|---|---|
| **2** | CUPS ALL-PURPOSE FLOUR |
| **2** | STICKS (1 CUP) SALTED BUTTER |
| **2** | LARGE EGG YOLKS |
| **2** | TO 3 TABLESPOONS ICE WATER |

**Filling**

| | |
|---|---|
| **1** | STICK (½ CUP) SALTED BUTTER |
| **4** | OUNCES UNSWEETENED BAKING CHOCOLATE |
| **2** | LARGE EGGS |
| **1** | CUP (PACKED) DARK BROWN SUGAR |
| **½** | CUP CORN SYRUP |
| **2** | TEASPOONS VANILLA EXTRACT |
| **1½** | CUPS PECANS, CHOPPED |

**Topping**

| | |
|---|---|
| **24** | PECAN HALVES |
| **½** | CUP HEAVY CREAM |
| **¼** | CUP GRANULATED SUGAR |
| **1** | TEASPOON VANILLA EXTRACT |

**1** Prepare pastry: In medium bowl, combine flour and butter with pastry cutter until dough resembles coarse meal. Add egg yolks and water, then mix with a fork just until dough can be shaped into a ball.

**2** Gather dough into a ball. Wrap tightly in plastic wrap or a plastic bag. Refrigerate until firm—about 1 hour.

**3** Prepare filling: In a 2-quart saucepan combine butter and chocolate, stirring constantly over low heat. Transfer to medium bowl and let cool for 5 minutes. With an electric mixer on medium speed, beat eggs into chocolate mixture. Add sugar, corn syrup, and vanilla, and blend on low speed until smooth. Fold in pecans.

**4** Preheat oven to 350°F.

**5** Assemble tartlets: On lightly floured counter or board, use a lightly floured rolling pin to roll out dough to ⅛-inch thickness. Using a 2½-inch fluted tartlet pan as a guide, cut dough ¼ inch around entire edge. Repeat with remaining dough. Lay dough rounds in tartlet pans and press in firmly.

**6** Fill pans ⅔ full of chocolate pecan filling. Place on baking sheet to catch any drips. Bake for 30 to 35 minutes, or until filling is set and does not look wet.

**7** While still warm, place a pecan half in center of each tartlet. Meanwhile, chill mixing bowl and beaters in freezer.

**8** Prepare topping: In a medium bowl with electric mixer set on high, beat cream, sugar, and vanilla until stiff peaks form. Do not overbeat. Transfer the whipped topping to a pastry bag fitted with a medium star tip, and pipe decorative topping onto each tartlet.

# METRIC CONVERSIONS

## DRY INGREDIENTS

| | |
|---|---|
| Baking powder/soda | 1 tsp. = 3 grams |
| Cornmeal | 1 cup = 150 grams |
| Cornstarch | ¼ cup = 30 grams |
| FLOUR | |
| All-purpose, unsifted | 1 cup = 120 grams |
| Cake or pastry, sifted | 1 cup = 100 grams |
| Whole-wheat, unsifted | 1 cup = 125 grams |
| Nuts, coarsely chopped | 1 cup = 140 grams |
| Herbs, dry | 1 tsp. = 2 grams |
| Rice, uncooked | 1 cup = 150 grams |
| Salt | 1 tsp. = 5 grams |
| Spices, ground | 1 tsp. = 2 grams |
| SUGAR | |
| Granulated | 1 tsp. = 5 grams |
| | 1 tbsp. = 15 grams |
| | 1 cup = 200 grams |
| Powdered | 1 cup = 110 grams |
| Brown, packed | 1 cup = 220 grams |

## FATS, OILS, AND CHEESE

| | |
|---|---|
| Butter | 8 tablespoons = |
| | ½ cup = 4 ounces = |
| | 125 grams |
| Shortening or lard | 1 cup = 250 grams |
| Vegetable oil | ¼ cup = 60 ml |
| Cheese, grated | 1 cup = 4 ounces = |
| | 120 grams |

## LIQUID MEASURES

1 tablespoon = 15 ml
1 fluid ounce = 30 ml
¼ cup = 60 ml
⅓ cup = 80 ml
½ cup = 125 ml
¾ cup = 185 ml
1 cup = 250 ml
1 quart = 1 liter

## WEIGHTS

1 ounce = 30 grams
1 pound = 450 grams
2.2 pounds = 1 kilogram

## FAHRENHEIT/CELSIUS CONVERSIONS

$9/5C + 32 = F$
$(F - 32)5/9 = C$

## OVEN TEMPERATURES

| °Fahrenheit | °Celsius |
|---|---|
| 250 (low oven) | 120 |
| 300 | 150 |
| 325 | 160 |
| 350 (moderate oven) | 175 |
| 400 | 200 |
| 450 | 230 |
| 500 (very hot oven) | 260 |

# INDEX